A PRACTICAL GUIDE FOR
TEACHING
SELF-DETERMINATION

SHARON FIELD

JIM MARTIN

ROBERT MILLER

MICHAEL WARD

MICHAEL WEHMEYER

Developed by the Division on Career Development and Transition · A Division of The Council for Exceptional Children
Published by The Council for Exceptional Children

Library of Congress Cataloging-in-Publication Data

A practical guide for teaching self-determination / Sharon Field . . .
   [et al.].
      p.   cm.
   "Developed by the Division on Career Development and Transition, a
division of the Council for Exceptional Children."
   Includes bibliographical references.
   ISBN 0-86586-301-6 (pbk.)
   1. Handicapped students—Education—United States—Handbooks,
manuals, etc. 2. Autonomy (Psychology)—Study and teaching—United
States—Handbooks, manuals, etc. 3. School-to-work transition—
United States—Handbooks, manuals, etc.   I. Field, Sharon.
II. Council for Exceptional Children. Division on Career
Development and Transition.
LC4031.P682   1998
371.9—dc21

                                                        97-36908
                                                            CIP

ISBN 0-86586-301-6

Stock No. P5231

Printed in the United States of America
10 9 8 7 6 5 4 3 2 1

Contents

Preface

This practitioner's guide to self-determination is targeted to K through 12 special education/special population instructors, work experience coordinators, vocational assessment personnel, guidance counselors, and other support services staff. Its purpose is to provide a practical guide to practices that promote self-determination. The guide addresses the legislative and research foundations for self-determination; terminology; assessment of self-determination; the relationship between career development, transition, and self-determination; self-determination methods, curricula, and materials; and self-determination in transition planning.

This guide uses a question-and-answer format to identify and respond to key topics practitioners need to address to promote student self-determination in their service settings. Although the strongest emphasis on self-determination has taken place in secondary and adult programs and services, early experiences are critical to developing knowledge, beliefs, and skills that lead to self-determination. Therefore, the guide takes a longitudinal approach to self-determination and discusses approaches to self-determination that are appropriate throughout a person's life span.

Curriculum and assessment resources available to educators and service providers are described throughout this guide along with appropriate contact information. In addition, an appendix includes an annotated bibliography of recent articles and books written on the topic of self-determination.

The Importance of Self-Determination

The purpose of this chapter is to

- Define self-determination and concepts related to self-determination, such as empowerment and self-advocacy.

- Describe why self-determination is important for students with disabilities.

What Is Self-Determination?

Mithaug (1991) observed that "in every school in this country, a few children succeed regardless of the instruction they receive. Teachers identify these students early, because they have purpose in their lives. They know what they like, what they can do, what they want, and how to get it. They are self-determined" (p. 1).

What does it mean to be self-determined? There is general consensus about the characteristics that are typical of self-determined people. These are evident in the most frequently cited definitions of self-determination. For example, in one of the earliest conceptualizations of self-determination as an educational outcome, Ward (1988) defined self-determination as referring to "both the attitudes which lead people to define goals for themselves and to their ability to take the initiative to achieve these goals" (p. 2). Ward identified the characteristics of self-actualization, assertiveness, creativity, pride, and self-advocacy as associated with self-determination. According to Ward, self-actualization is necessary to achieve one's full potential. Assertiveness is needed to act in a self-confident manner and to express needs clearly and directly. Creativity helps the individual act in ways that exceed stereotyped roles and expectations. Pride contributes to the individual's ability to recognize his or her abilities and contributions to society. Skills in self-advocacy are needed to ensure access to the services and benefits needed to facilitate the achievement of one's full potential.

Field and Hoffman (1994) defined self-determination as "one's ability to define and achieve goals based on a foundation of knowing and valuing oneself" (p. 136). Their model of self-determination addresses cognitive, affective, and behavioral factors that promote self-determination. It has five major components: (1) know yourself, (2) value yourself, (3) plan, (4) act, and (5) experience outcomes and learn.

Wehmeyer (1996) defined self-determination as "acting as the primary causal agent in one's life and making choices and decisions regarding one's quality of life free from undue external influence or interference" (p. 22). According to Wehmeyer, individuals are self-determined if their actions reflect four essential characteristics: (1) the individual acted autonomously, (2) the behaviors were self-regulated, (3) the individual initiated and responded to events in a psychologically empowered manner, and (4) the individual acted in a self-realizing manner. These essential characteristics emerge based on the acquisition of a set of component elements of self-determined behavior, including choice- and decision-making, problem-solving, self-management, and self-advocacy skills and adaptive perceptions of control, efficacy, and self-awareness. It is at the level of component elements that instruction occurs.

To summarize, self-determination is a combination of skills, knowledge, and beliefs that enable a person to engage in goal-directed, self-regulated, autonomous behavior. An understanding of one's strengths and limitations together with a belief in oneself as capable and effective are essential to self-determination. When acting on the basis of these skills and attitudes, individuals have greater ability to take control of their lives and assume the role of successful adults in our society.

What Are Some of the Characteristics of Self-Determined People?

Martin and Marshall (1995) summarized the "evolving definition of self-determination in the special education literature" as describing individuals who:

> know how to choose—they know what they want and how to get it. From an awareness of personal needs, self-determined individuals choose goals, then doggedly pursue them. This involves asserting an individual's presence, making his or her needs known, evaluating progress toward meeting goals, adjusting performance, and creating unique approaches to solve problems. (p. 147)

As illustrated by this description, self-determined people exhibit a set of characteristics that enable them to fulfill roles typically associated with adulthood. There is wide agreement on some, if not most, of the characteristics of self-determination. The following have been proposed across multiple models or frameworks as characteristics of self-determined individuals:

- Awareness of personal preferences, interests, strengths, and limitations.
- Ability to differentiate between wants and needs.
- Ability to make choices based on preferences, interests, wants, and needs.
- Ability to consider multiple options and to anticipate consequences for decisions.
- Ability to initiate and take action when needed.
- Ability to evaluate decisions based on the outcomes of previous decisions and to revise future decisions accordingly.
- Ability to set and work toward goals.
- Problem-solving skills.
- A striving for independence while recognizing interdependence with others.
- Self-advocacy skills.
- Ability to self-regulate behavior.
- Self-evaluation skills.
- Independent performance and adjustment skills.
- Persistence.
- Ability to use communication skills such as negotiation, compromise, and persuasion to reach goals.
- Ability to assume responsibility for actions and decisions.
- Self-confidence.
- Pride.
- Creativity.

What Factors Have Influenced the Current Focus on Self-Determination?

The self-determination initiative in special education emerged as a result of several factors. First, there has been a changing view of disability in the United States and, as a result, an increase in visibility of individuals with disabilities. This increased visibility came about as the logical extension of the independent living, normalization, and self-advocacy movements of the preceding decades (Ward, 1996). The Rehabilitation Act Amendments of 1992 captured the essence of the reconceptualization of disability, stating that "disability is a natural part of the human experience and in no way diminishes the right of an individual to live independently, enjoy self-determination, make choices, contribute to society, pursue meaningful careers, and enjoy full inclusion and integration in the economic, political, social, cultural, and educational mainstream of American society" [Section 2 (a)(3)(A–F)]. People with disabilities are more visible and more vocal than ever before, and they are increasingly demanding more control and choice in their lives.

The increased visibility of people with disabilities in all aspects of our society has contributed to the growing civil and legal protections that prohibit discrimination based on disability, such as the Americans with Disabilities Act, the Fair Housing Amendments, Section 504 of the Rehabilitation Act, and the Individuals with Disabilities Education Act. Such legislation enables individuals with disabilities to participate more fully in their communities, and this in turn increases the importance of providing students with educational experiences that promote self-determination so that they can take advantage of their rights. Thus, in addition to becoming more visible, people with disabilities now have greater protection against discrimination and segregation. It is important they also have the ability to take advantage of these protections.

A third factor that has contributed to the emergence of the self-determination movement has been the publication of results of a number of follow-up and follow-along studies examining the adult experiences of youth with disabilities after graduation. These studies have consistently indicated that postsecondary outcomes for students with disabilities are not as positive as those of their nondisabled peers (Chadsey-Rusch, Rusch, & O'Reilly, 1991) and do not lead to satisfying, financially secure lives. These findings have convinced researchers and educators alike that, while we have considerable knowledge about how to prepare young people with disabilities for adulthood, we need to continue our search for additional practices. Among such practices are the promotion of self-determination and increased student involvement in educational planning, decision making, and program implementation as a means to begin teaching self-determination.

Why Is Self-Determination Important for Students with Disabilities?

Although emphasis on self-determination is important for individuals without disabilities, it is more critical to emphasize self-determination for people with disabilities in order to shatter the many pervasive stereotypes that portray members of this population as being unable to practice self-determination (Ward, 1988). For centuries, persons with disabilities have been treated as objects of pity and fear. In addition to the stigma of disability, the literature continues to document poor employment and independent living outcomes experienced by people with disabilities (Sitlington, Frank, & Carson, 1993; Wagner, D'Amico, Marder, Newman, & Blackorby, 1992).

The importance of self-determination in the transition process has been affirmed in the Division on Career Development and Transition position statement on the transition of youth with disabilities to adult life (Halpern, 1994). According to Halpern, a major component of transition must be "an emerging sense of student empowerment which eventually enhances student self-determination within the transition process. . ." (p. 118). The statement contends that if transition planning is to be successful for individual students, they must become empowered with respect to their own transition planning. Since student needs and interests are the basis for transition planning, student selection of future goals is critical in this process.

What Factors Are Important in the Development of Self-Determination for Children and Youth with Disabilities?

Ward (1988) suggested that "acquiring the personal characteristics which lead to self-determination is a developmental process that begins in early childhood and continues throughout adult life" (p. 2). Self-determination is too often portrayed as simply a transition service. However, unless students with disabilities acquire and develop the various attitudes and abilities associated with self-determination throughout their educational careers, from early childhood to high school, they will not be prepared to become self-determined young adults.

Doll, Sands, Wehmeyer, and Palmer (1996) reviewed the literature reporting the development of various component elements of self-determined behavior, summarized the self-determination skills typically present at each of four school ages, and made recommendations regarding instruction that can be used in the school and home. A brief description of important factors at each of the four stages (early childhood, early elementary, late elementary, and secondary) follows. Recommended instructional strategies are summarized in Figure 1-1.

Early Childhood. During early childhood (ages 2–5), children exhibit the building blocks of self-determined behavior. They can recognize and express their preferences and make choices based on a restricted awareness of options. However, their choices and preferences rarely relate to either personal goals or aspirations, and instead reflect their present wants. At this age, children have inaccurate and overly optimistic estimates of their own abilities and an egocentric social perspective, which limits their ability to direct the behaviors of others to achieve desired ends. Finally, young children do not systematically or spontaneously revise their choice of actions based on the success or failure of that choice.

Instructional emphasis during early childhood involves providing opportunities for children to make choices by offering options, assisting children to recognize alternatives, and restricting choices that are possibly harmful. Doll and colleagues (1996) suggested that "adults can encourage a preschooler's emergent understanding of the links between choices and later opportunities by revisiting the choices the child has made in the very recent past, helping the child identify the consequences of these choices, and discussing plans for future choices" (p. 82). Educators can also promote goal-directed behavior by encouraging students to make plans and abide by them during the school day. They can promote perspective taking by asking students to think about how others feel about certain circumstances.

Early Elementary Years. During early elementary years, students can identify, and are more likely to implement, solutions to problems that complement their abilities. They are able to generalize solutions from one problem to future problems, and their more mature perspective-taking skills enable them to exert more control over their social context. However, at

FIGURE 1-1
School and Family-Based Interventions to
Support the Development of Self-Determination

Early Childhood (Ages 2–5)

- Provide opportunities to make structured choices, such as, "Do you want to wear the blue shirt or the red shirt?" Extend choices across food, clothing, activity, and other choices.

- Provide opportunities to generate choices that are both positive and negative, such as, "We have 10 more minutes. What could we do?" and "You spilled your milk. What could you do to clean it up?"

- Provide formative and constructive feedback on the consequences of choices made in the recent past, such as, "When you pushed hard on the pencil it broke. What might you want to do the next time?" and "When you used an angry voice, I didn't do what you wanted. What could you do differently?"

- Provide opportunities for planning activities that are pending, such as, "You need to choose a dress to wear to the wedding," or "Decide what kind of sandwich you want to take for lunch tomorrow."

- Provide opportunities to self-evaluate task performance by comparing their work to a model. Point out what they've done that's like the model, such as, "Look, you used nice colors too, just like this one," and "Do you see that you both drew the man from the side?"

- Ask directive questions so that the child compares his or her performance to a model, such as, "Are all of your toys in the basket, too?" or "I'll know you're ready for the story when you are sitting on your mat with your legs crossed, your hands on your knees, and your eyes on me."

Early Elementary (Ages 6–8)

- Provide opportunities to choose from among several different strategies for a task, such as, "Will you remember your spelling words better if you write them out, say them to yourself, or test yourself?" or "What is the easiest way for you to figure out what this word means?"

- Ask children to reconsider choices they've made in the recent past, in light of those choices' subsequent consequences, such as, "This morning you decided to spend your lunch money on the comic. Now it's lunchtime and you're hungry. What decision do you wish you'd made?" or "I remember when you decided to leave your coat in your locker. What happened because you made that decision?"

- Encourage children to "think aloud" with you, saying the steps that they are taking to complete a task or solve a problem, such as, "Tell me what you're thinking in your head while you try to figure out what the word means," or "You've lost your house key. What are you thinking to yourself while you decide what to do?"

- Provide opportunities for students to talk about how they learn, such as, "Is it easier for you to tell me what you want by saying it or by writing it down?" or "Do you remember better if you study for a test all at once or a little bit on several different days?" Help students test out their answers.

- Provide opportunities for students to systematically evaluate their work, such as, "Here's a very neat paper, and here's your paper. Is your paper as neat as this one? What are the differences between this paper and yours? How are they alike?"

- Help students set simple goals for themselves and check to see whether they are reaching them, such as, "You said you want to read two books this week. How much of a book have you read so far? Let's color in your goal sheet so you can see how much you've done."

Note. From Sands, D. J., & Wehmeyer, M. L. (Eds.). (1996). *Self-determination across the life span: Independence and choice for people with disabilities.* Baltimore: Paul H. Brookes, pp. 8–9. Reprinted with permission.

FIGURE 1-1 (continued)

Late Elementary (Ages 9–11)

- Provide guidance in systematic analyses of decisions: writing the problem at the top of a sheet of paper, listing all possible choices, and sketching out the benefits and cost of each choice.

- Use the same systematic structure to analyze past decisions now that their consequences are evident, such as, "You were angry at Jo for teasing you, and so you punched her in the cheek. Now you have to sit out at recess for a week. What are some other things that you could have done instead? What might have happened then?"

- Provide opportunities for students to commit to personal or academic goals: writing the goal down and storing it in a safe place, revisiting the goal periodically to reflect on progress toward it, listing optional steps to take toward the goal, and trying out the steps and reflecting on their success.

- Provide opportunities to systematically analyze adult perspectives, such as the point of view of the volleyball coach when a student is late to every game or the perspective of the librarian when a student returns a book that is dirty and torn. Help the student guess what the adult is thinking and feeling and what might be done as a result.

- Provide opportunities for students to evaluate task performance in affectively "safe" ways: identifying weaknesses and strengths in performance, reflecting on ways to improve performance, trying out some ways, and reevaluating performance to check for improvement. For example, "You got a lower grade than you wanted on your research paper. What steps did you take to make it a really strong paper? What steps did you leave out? What might you do now to make it even better?"

Secondary (Ages 12–18)

- Provide opportunities for students to make decisions that have important impact on their day-to-day activities, such as academic goals, careers to explore, schedules to keep, diet and sleep habits, and others.

- Make it easy for students to see the link between goals they set for themselves and the daily decisions that they make, such as, "You made a point of going to bed early last night, and now I see you earned a 95 on today's quiz. Going to bed on time seems to be helping you meet your goal of higher grades this semester," or "You've set aside half of every paycheck, and now you have $625 in the bank. It won't be long before you have enough to buy the computer you want."

- Provide guidance in breaking students' long-term goals into a number of short-term objectives. Lead students through planning activities to determine steps to take to progress toward these goals. For example, help a student break the goal of a higher math grade into smaller objectives of rechecking math homework before handing it in, practicing the math problems on nights before the test, asking questions whenever something isn't clear.

- Assist the student in realistically recognizing and accepting weaknesses in key skills. You might say, for example, "It's hard for you to do your math problems without making mistakes in your math facts. What are some parts of math that you're good at? What could you do to get around the reality that you don't remember math facts well?"

- Assist students in requesting academic and social supports from teachers. Say, for example, "You'd like Mrs. Green to let you have some extra time to complete the weekly quiz. How will you ask her for that?" or "You think you'd do better work if your boss would let you use a note pad to jot down the orders. What can you do to ask for that?"

this age students still fail to correct the course of a plan of action based on the outcome of that action, and, although they can set some basic goals and work toward them over brief time periods, they require considerable adult support to complete such actions.

Instructional emphasis during these years should continue to be placed on the use of multiple strategies to achieve a solution to a problem and the presence of various options for choice and decision making. Teachers should help students recognize matches between their unique abilities and various strategies or options. Teachers can encourage students of this age to revisit decisions based on the information gained by their action, and to formulate a revised approach if necessary. Early elementary age students should be assisted in evaluating their own work to promote self-regulation, and they can practice and understand rule-based decision making (Doll et al., 1996, p. 81).

Late Elementary Years. During the late elementary years (ages 9–11), students begin to set personal goals spontaneously and apply those goals to their actions. They are able to recognize when a specific course of action is not working and can correct that course. These students are beginning to understand the differential effects of effort, talent, and luck or chance on an outcome and can apply this understanding to selecting appropriate strategies. What these students lack, according to Doll and colleagues (1996), is "the structure for systematic analysis of the consequences of the various options from which they choose" (p. 82). In essence, students of this age cannot articulate a clear reason or rationale for decisions, even though they can make decisions that are similar to adult decisions.

Instructional emphasis should focus on supporting students in making decisions, including providing support in listing options, identifying consequences, and weighing costs. In this process, students can revisit past decisions and identify alternative courses of actions if warranted. Beyond this, however, students at this age should be assisted to use their emerging decision-making skills to set goals for their personal and school life and to monitor their progress toward these goals. With adult guidance, students can self-evaluate their needs based on their strengths and weaknesses.

Secondary Years. In the secondary years (12 and over), students can demonstrate decision-making skills similar in most respects to those of adults, generalize successful problem-solving strategies from one situation to another, focus on long-term goals and objectives, and revise plans to achieve these goals. These students are more able to assume control over their lives, can provide an increasing level of informed consent, and can use their perspective-taking skills to negotiate and compromise on important issues. In fact, the primary barrier to effective self-determined behavior at this stage, other than opportunity, is the adolescent's tendency toward emotionality. Instruction at this age should emphasize increased responsibility for decision making, planning, goal setting, and self-regulated learning. Students will still require support to analyze their decisions systematically and critically evaluate the information they use to make decisions, as well as overcome the impulse to act on emotions as opposed to a plan or goal.

This picture of the development and acquisition of self-determined behavior depends as much on the teacher or other adults to structure the environment and learning experiences to support the student's development as it does on the student himself or herself. Students who have not been provided instructional opportunities in early childhood and elementary years will not be able to step in and function in the manner described for adolescents. Certainly the student's level of disability will impact the degree to which he or she can independently achieve each of the milestones represented. However, with adequate accommodation and supports, most students can achieve some, if not all, of the skills identified and take more control in their lives.

Why Is Self-Determination Important for Transition and Career Development?

Sarason (1990) stated that one major goal of education is to "produce responsible, self-sufficient citizens who possess the self-esteem, initiative, skills, and wisdom to continue individual growth and pursue knowledge" (p. 163). The purpose of transition services is to provide students with the skills and beliefs they need to achieve self-sufficiency in where they work, live, and play. It is evident from follow-up studies that too many students with disabilities are not self-sufficient, independent, or autonomous when they leave public schools. According to Martin, Marshall, Maxson, and Jerman (1993), "All too often these students are not taught how to self-manage their own lives before they are thrust into the cold water of post-school reality" (p. 4).

If students with disabilities are to succeed and become self-sufficient as young adults, they need more than job or daily living skills. They need to become self-determined. Wehmeyer and Schwartz (1995) conducted a follow-up study of 80 students with cognitive and learning disabilities to determine the impact of self-determination on their postschool lives. Students' self-determination was measured before they left school, and the sample was divided into high and low self-determination groups. Members of the high self-determination group were more likely to maintain a savings or checking account and be employed for pay. Students who earned the highest wages out of high school had significantly higher self-determination scores, and individual components of self-determination contributed significantly to the students' wages per hour. Throughout the study, youths with high self-determination scores consistently did better than their peers 1 year out of school.

Not only does self-determination contribute to more positive adult outcomes, but being self-determined contributes to an enhanced quality of life. Wehmeyer and Schwartz (in press) measured the self-determination and quality of life of 50 adults with cognitive disabilities, all of whom lived in group homes. Of several factors, including age, intelligence scores, measures of life choices, and life satisfaction, only self-determination predicted whether an individual had a higher quality of life.

What Is the Relationship Between Self-Determination, Self-Advocacy, and Empowerment?

Self-determination, self-advocacy, and empowerment are intertwined concepts, so much so that they are sometimes used interchangeably. It is important both to understand the ways in which they are linked and to distinguish between them.

As discussed in Chapter 4, *self-advocacy* refers, literally, to advocating on one's own behalf. To advocate means to speak up or defend a cause or person, and self-advocacy skills include being assertive, knowing your rights, speaking up, and negotiating. According to Lehr and Taylor (1986), self-advocacy means "being able to speak for yourself, to make decisions for yourself, to know what your rights are and how to 'stick up' for yourself when your rights are being violated or diminished. It also means being able to help others who cannot speak for themselves" (p. 3).

Thus, through instruction in self-advocacy, a person can work on behalf of himself or herself or on behalf of a group. There is a growing movement across the United States in which people with disabilities organize and run self-advocacy or self-help groups to provide a vehicle for personal and systemic advocacy (Ward, 1996).

Self-determination, as discussed earlier, refers to the skills and attitudes that enable a person to gain more control over his or her life. Among those skills are self-advocacy skills.

Both self-advocacy skills and self-determination skills lead to *empowerment*, which has been defined as "an intentional, ongoing process, centered in the local community, involving mutual respect, critical reflection, caring, and group participation, through which people who are lacking in an equal share of valued resources gain greater access to and control over those resources" (Cornell Empowerment and Family Project, 1990). Empowerment is the outcome of a process that is centered in the local community and encompasses integration and inclusion as implied outcomes. It is based on the philosophical assumption that all people are worthy of respect and being valued, independent of issues related to ability or disability, financial or material status, and racial or ethnic background.

Empowerment exists at a community level, but it also applies to the individual level. It is individualized, goal oriented, and based on action and analysis. At the root of empowerment, however, is control over resources—be they monetary, social, or otherwise—and the exercise of power in one's life. Unlike self-advocacy and self-determination, empowerment cannot be taught. However, as a result of learning self-advocacy and other self-determination skills, an individual may become empowered or have an empowering experience.

CONCLUSION

For years, many disenfranchised groups, including people with disabilities, have complained about not being given the power to control their own destiny. The self-determination initiative for students with disabilities is a response to this call. The outcome of instruction in self-determination is, ultimately, to empower the individual to assume control over his or her life.

REFERENCES

Chadsey-Rusch, J., Rusch, F., & O'Reilly, M. F. (1991). Transition from school to integrated communities. *Remedial and Special Education, 12*, 23–33. (ERIC Document Reproduction Service No. EJ 439 554)

Cornell Empowerment and Family Project (1990). *Networking: A bulletin on empowerment and family support.* Ithaca, NY: Author.

Doll, B., Sands, D. J., Wehmeyer, M. L., & Palmer, S. (1996). Promoting the development and acquisition of self-determined behavior. In D. J. Sands & M. L. Wehmeyer (Eds.), *Self-determination across the life span: Independence and choice for people with disabilities,* (pp. 63–88). Baltimore: Paul H. Brookes.

Field, S., & Hoffman, A. (1994). Development of a model for self-determination. *Career Development for Exceptional Individuals, 17*, 159–169. (ERIC Document Reproduction Service No. EJ 497 597)

Halpern, A. S. (1994). The transition of youth with disabilities to adult life: A position statement of the Division on Career Development and Transition. *Career Development for Exceptional Individuals, 17*, 115–124. (ERIC Document Reproduction Service No. EJ 497 593)

Lehr, S., & Taylor, S. J. (1986). *Roots and wings: A manual about self-advocacy.* (Available from the Federation for Special Needs, 95 Berkeley Street, Suite 104, Boston, MA 02116).

Martin, J. E., & Marshall, L. H. (1995). ChoiceMaker: A comprehensive self-determination transition program. *Intervention in School and Clinic, 30*, 147–156. (ERIC Document Reproduction Service No. EJ 497 548)

Martin, J. E., Marshall, L. H., Maxson, L., & Jerman, P. (1993). *Self-directed IEP: Teacher's manual.* Colorado Springs: University of Colorado Center for Educational Research.

Mithaug, D. E. (1991). *Self-determined kids: Raising satisfied and successful children.* Lexington, MA: Lexington Books.

Sarason, S. B. (1990). *The predictable failure of educational reform.* San Francisco: Jossey-Bass.

Sitlington, P. L., Frank, A. R., & Carson, R. (1993). Adult adjustment among high school graduates with mild disabilities. *Exceptional Children, 59,* 221–233. (ERIC Reproduction Service Document No. EJ 457 401)

Wagner, M., D'Amico, R, Marder, C., Newman, L., & Blackorby, J. (1992). *What happens next: Trends in postschool outcomes of youth with disabilities.* Menlo Park, CA: SRI International.

Ward, M. J. (1988). The many facets of self-determination. *National Information Center for Children and Youth with Handicaps transition summary, 5,* 2–3.

Ward, M. J. (1996). Coming of age in the age of self-determination: A historical and personal perspective. In D. J. Sands & M. L. Wehmeyer (Eds.), *Self-determination across the life span: Independence and choice for people with disabilities* (pp. 1–14). Baltimore: Paul H. Brookes.

Wehmeyer, M. L. (1996). Self-determination as an educational outcome: Why is it important to children, youth and adults with disabilities? In D. J. Sands & M. L. Wehmeyer (Eds.), *Self-determination across the life span: Independence and choice for people with disabilities* (pp. 15–34). Baltimore: Paul H. Brookes.

Wehmeyer, M. L., & Schwartz, M. (1995). *Self-determination and positive adult outcomes: A follow-up study of youth with mental retardation and learning disabilities. Exceptional Children, 63,* 245–255.

Wehmeyer, M. L., & Schwartz, M. (in press). *The relationship between self-determination and quality of life. Exceptional Children, 63.*

2

Student Involvement in the IEP and Transition Process

The purpose of this chapter is to

- Discuss the importance of student involvement in the transition planning process.

- Describe specific strategies to prepare students for participation in educational and transition planning.

- Identify strategies to increase student participation in educational and transition planning meetings.

- Identify ways that parents, teachers, and administrators can support students during the development and implementation of educational and transition plans.

SELF-DETERMINATION AND STUDENT LEADERSHIP OF THE IEP AND TRANSITION PROCESS

Why Is Student Involvement in Transition Planning and the IEP Process So Important?

Put yourself in the shoes of a 16-year-old student receiving special education services. Teachers, parents, and school support staff meet to discuss your progress toward meeting your past educational goals, review assessment information, discuss your strengths and weaknesses, establish new goals for next year, and determine where you will go to school. You may not even know that this meeting is being held until it is over. Then a teacher or maybe your mother comes to tell you that next year you are going to be in a different school. How would this make you feel? Would it make you feel as if you had no control over your life? Would it make you feel unimportant? Would it make you wonder whether anyone wants your input? Would it help you learn how to become engaged and a part of your own education?

That is why active student involvement in the individualized education program (IEP) process is so important. It is more than symbolic, in that a student's active participation in and leadership of his or her own IEP meeting shows active engagement when she or he says, "Hey! This is my life and this is my education. I know what my interests, skills, and limits are. Here are my goals, and I believe I need these supports to help achieve them." Can you imagine students making a more serious claim for wanting to become engaged and involved in their own education?

Active student participation and leadership of the IEP process are also excellent means to teach crucial self-determination skills. Educational policy leaders contend that learning self-determination skills is the ultimate goal for students with disabilities (Ward & Halloran, 1993). Mithaug (1996) believes that our society, and in particular our schools, must optimize self-determination by increasing students' self-determination skills and providing opportunities for self-determination. There is no better place than the IEP process to begin teaching and providing opportunities for self-determination. Powers (1996a) found that school staff and parents want students to participate actively in their own IEP meetings. Finally, when students establish their own goals, it is a powerful behavior change strategy (Johnson & Graham, 1990; Locke, Shaw, Saari, & Latham, 1981).

What Self-Determination Skills Are Taught Through Students' Learning How to Lead Their Own IEP and Transition Process?

Teaching students how to actively participate in and lead their own IEP process helps them gain important self-determination knowledge and skills (Martin & Huber Marshall, 1995). These include

- Self-awareness (ability to identify interests, strengths, and limits and to understand disabilities).

- Self-advocacy (ability to know rights, determine supports, and conduct own affairs).

- Self-efficacy (belief that one can achieve goals and attain outcomes).

- Decision-making (ability to set goals and standards, generate strategies, and complete a plan).

- Independent performance (ability to complete tasks on time, use self-management strategies, perform tasks to a standard, and follow through on plans).

- Self-evaluation (ability to compare performance to a standard and evaluate effectiveness of plan).

- Adjustment (ability to change parts of a plan that are not working).

Each of these seven constructs is a part of the IEP process. Instead of educators being solely responsible for making the IEP process work, students can be taught to become involved in the process and at the same time learn crucial self-determination skills.

What Does the Individuals with Disabilities Education Act (IDEA) Say About Student Involvement in the IEP Transition Process?

According to IDEA, a statement of transition services must be provided in each student's IEP beginning no later than age 14, and earlier if appropriate. The regulations implementing Part B of IDEA clearly state that the public agency (i.e., school district) must invite students to attend their IEP meetings if the purpose is the consideration of transition services. Additionally, IDEA states that student transition activities must be based upon the student's interests and preferences. If the student does not attend the IEP meeting, other steps must be taken to ensure that his or her interests and preferences are considered.

When Should Students Get Involved in Their IEP Process?

The extent of student participation in IEP meetings is a function of the student's age and willingness and the school's philosophy and policy. Academy School District in Colorado Springs, Colorado, for instance, recently developed a district-wide, board-approved policy addressing this issue (Martin, Huber Marshall, & Maxson, 1993). In this policy statement, students receiving special education services observe and participate in their IEP staffings starting about the second or third grade. By the time students are half way through middle school, they learn to manage their IEP meetings to the greatest extent possible. This will continue through the high school years. Of course, student involvement in the IEP meeting during the early years is dependent upon the activities taking place in the meeting and what the team believes is appropriate. Crucial to the success of this policy is teaching students what the IEP process is, what they need to do during their IEP meetings, and what they need to do to help implement the IEP.

High school students who have not been participants at previous IEP meetings are frequently reluctant to attend their first meeting. To help alleviate students' fears, peers can be asked to discuss or role play their experiences of their IEP meetings. In addition, the teacher can show a video modeling student behavior at an IEP meeting. Also, students can be taught the language, purpose, and behaviors needed to facilitate an effective meeting. Finally, parents should be encouraged to support their son's or daughter's involvement.

Before the IEP meeting, the student and teacher need to meet to determine the student's role. Some students will be sufficiently skillful to direct their own IEP meetings, others will need assistance. Those who need assistance may wish to co-chair their meeting with a teacher or other support person. The support person can help facilitate the flow of the meeting and assist with any difficult portions.

What Should a Student-Centered IEP Transition Meeting Look Like?

Rather than viewing the IEP meeting as a boring, bureaucratic necessity, more and more students, parents, and educators now consider it an opportunity to celebrate a student's education. To foster this feeling of celebration, some educators provide instruction for students in skills that will allow them to increase their involvement in educational and transition planning meetings—for example, how to schedule their own meeting, invite the participants, send reminder notices, prepare refreshments, dress in clothes appropriate for a formal meeting, speak up for themselves, and actively participate in the meeting.

The way in which he or she is involved in the meeting will depend on the needs and preferences of the individual student. It may be appropriate for many students to sit at the head of the table and chair the meeting. A coach, usually the teacher who assisted the student to develop IEP meeting skills and prepare for the meeting, will usually sit next to the student. The student should have a script or prompts, discussion points, and notes in front of him or her to share with the group, just like the other team members. With assistance provided by a coach if needed, the student can facilitate or lead the discussion needed to complete the various sections of the IEP meeting.

Who Is Required to Participate in the IEP Transition Meeting?

An IEP meeting at which transition services are discussed *must* include the following participants: an administrative representative from the education agency (usually the building principal or special education supervisor); the student's teacher; one or both of the student's parents; the student; and other individuals at the discretion of the student, parent, or education agency (e.g., related services personnel, friends, or general education teacher).

As mentioned previously, the education agency *must* make an extra effort to invite the student to the IEP meeting at which transition services will be discussed. The agency must also invite a representative from any other agency (e.g., vocational rehabilitation, developmental disabilities, etc.) that is likely to assist with providing or paying for transition services. The intent of this requirement is to get adult service agencies that provide ongoing support involved with students prior to their leaving school.

Should Persons Other Than Those Who Are Required Participate in the IEP Transition Meeting? If So, Who?

Others can be invited to participate in the meeting or preplanning activities if it would benefit the individual student. Teachers and parents may want to encourage the student to invite important people in his or her life who could make contributions or provide support at the meeting. This may include a best friend, girlfriend or boyfriend, coworker, grandparent, or sibling. These significant others can discuss the student's progress toward past goals, help shape future goals, and provide support not only before and during the meeting, but afterward when goals are being attained. Depending on the needs of the individual student and the time allotment for the meeting, it may be helpful to ask the student to interview some of these individuals prior to the meeting to gain their input, rather than having a group that is too large and unwieldy at the IEP meeting.

What Pre-Planning Activities Should Occur, If Any?

Several preplanning activities may occur to help make the IEP meeting a meaningful experience for the student and others in attendance. These pre-planning activities should include teaching the student skills to participate in and lead the meeting, conducting interviews with friends and family members to determine interests, and undertaking experiential activities so the students can learn about their own interests, skills, and limits.

PREPARATION FOR STUDENT LEADERSHIP OF THE IEP AND TRANSITION PROCESS

What Do Students Need to Do to Learn to Participate in and Lead Their IEP Transition Process?

Active student participation in the IEP process is dependent upon learning IEP meeting skills. Powers (1996a) reported poor outcomes when students simply attend their meetings without any prior instruction in what to do. In these situations:

- Students did not understand IEP transition meeting language.

- Students did not understand the purpose behind the meeting, nor did they know their role.

- Participants did not respond to what the students said.

Students need to learn IEP meeting behaviors and collect information about their own interests, skills, and barriers across the various transition areas in order to actively participate in and perhaps lead their own IEP meetings. Martin, Huber Marshall, Maxson, Jerman, and Miller (1996) suggested that students need to learn the following 11 steps to actively participate in and manage their IEP meetings:

1. Begin meeting by stating purpose.

2. Introduce everyone.

3. Review past goals and performance.

4. Ask for others' feedback.

5. State your school and transition goals.

6. Ask questions if you do not understand.

7. Deal with differences in opinion.

8. State what support you will need.

9. Summarize your goals.

10. Close meeting by thanking everyone.

11. Work on IEP goals all year.

Participating in and managing the flow of the IEP meeting is important, but it is only a portion of what students need to successfully participate in their own staffing. Students must also bring into the meeting knowledge of their interests, skills, and barriers across the four different transition areas (i.e., education; employment; personal and daily living; and housing and community participation). The team then merges student information with the input provided from other meeting participants to prioritize goals.

How Can Students Learn These IEP Leadership Skills?

Asking a student to attend an IEP transition meeting without any prior instruction in what the process is about, his or her role, and expected outcomes is setting the stage for a bad experience (Powers, 1996a) that (a) the student likely will not enjoy, (b) meeting participants most likely will view as patronizing, and (c) does not fulfill the goal of helping the student to make meaningful plans for his or her future.

To ensure a successful meeting and make the IEP process a learning experience in which the student acquires generalizable self-determination skills, the student needs to learn a set of skills. Several curriculum lesson packages used alone or in combination are available to help teach IEP meeting behavior. Six curricula that teach students IEP meeting skills are described briefly here. Chapter 5 describes these and other lesson packages in more detail.

Become Your Own Expert (Carpenter, 1995). High school students with learning disabilities use this curriculum to develop the self-advocacy skills to have an active role in their IEP and transition planning process. Through the use of this lesson package, students learn to understand their disabilities, strengths, weaknesses, needed accommodations, and rights.

Next S.T.E.P. (Halpern et al., 1997). This lesson package teaches students to take charge of their personal transition planning meetings through 16 lessons that help students learn to:

- Understand the nature and purpose of transition planning.
- Identify opportunities for self-exploration and self-evaluation across the different transition areas.
- Develop goals.
- Prepare for their planning meetings.
- Follow up on the commitments made at meetings.

An accompanying videotape for students, parents, and educators complements the process covered in the lessons.

The Self-Advocacy Strategy (Van Reusen, Bos, Schumaker, & Deshler, 1994). This curriculum provides instruction in a motivation strategy students can use when preparing for and participating in an educational conference, including the IEP and transition planning meetings. The strategy steps teach students how to get organized before a conference and how to communicate during the meeting. Students use the acronym "I PLAN" to remember the five strategy steps. Each letter of "I PLAN" cues the student to use a step. The five steps are to (1) inventory, (2) provide your inventory information, (3) listen and respond, (4) ask questions, and (5) name your goals.

The Self-Directed IEP (Martin, Huber Marshall, Maxson, Jerman, & Miller, 1996). This lesson package teaches students 11 steps they need to actively participate and manage their IEP and transition meeting. In addition, it shows students how to disclose their interests, skills, and limits and how to build necessary support to reach their goals. Students complete in-class exercises in their workbook after viewing two videos. The first video, *The Self-Directed IEP in Action*, shows students who have managed their IEP meeting teaching other students how to do it. It also shows a group of students talking about what self-determination means to them. The second video, *The Self-Directed IEP*, shows a student leading his own IEP meeting through flashbacks while talking to a friend who was invited to attend her next IEP meeting. This lesson package is part of the *ChoiceMaker Self-Determination Curriculum and Lessons*.

A Student's Guide to the IEP (McGahee-Kovac, 1995) and Helping Students Develop Their IEPs (National Information Center for Children and Youth with Disabilities, 1995). The National Information Center for Children and Youth with Disabilities recently published these materials to help facilitate student involvement in their IEP process. The guide is an easy-to-read booklet that explains the basic aspects of the IEP process and how to be a part of the process. Included is an audiotape on which students describe their experiences in being an active participant in their IEP process and what it meant to them. The second booklet is a guide for parents and teachers to help students become involved in their IEP process. An audiotape of parents and teachers discussing how they helped students become active IEP participants is also included.

Take Charge for the Future (Powers, 1996b). This instructional package teaches students to lead a transition meeting, including how to share their dreams about the future, discuss their goals and needed supports, and facilitate the meeting to gain support from others. The student manual gives an overview of the typical agenda, provides tips on how the student should act, and provides examples of agendas students can read. Included, too, is a discussion on assertiveness methods and how to prepare parents and others for the meeting.

Whose Future Is It Anyway? (Wehmeyer & Kelchner, 1995) This instructional package provides students the opportunity to acquire the knowledge and confidence to take part in the transition process as equal partners. The package emphasizes disability as a part of the human condition and stresses that students need to be aware of their own learning abilities and needs. Each session teaches students something they can use in their transition meeting. Students learn

- To write and track goals.
- To identify community resources.
- How informed consent affects them.
- To participate in a meeting.

Students independently read through a set of humorous lessons and complete various exercises to help learn the points associated with each lesson.

What Are the Roles of Teachers, Administrators, and Parents in the IEP Process?

The emphasis on a team approach to development of transition services is a key point in the IDEA legislation. The emphasis in this chapter is on how to ensure that students are involved as active team participants. It is important to note that this does not negate or decrease the importance of the other team participants. In fact, it may accentuate the need for active involvement by other IEP team members as well as the student. Active participation by all team members can help to support involvement by students.

Teachers, administrators, and parents play unique roles, yet share many common ones.

Roles Shared by Teachers, Administrators, and Parents

- Direct statements to the student.
- Look at the student when talking about him or her.
- Consider the student as the facilitator of the IEP meeting, if this is a role the student is prepared to assume.
- Use words and gestures the student can understand.
- If a teacher is coaching the student through the IEP process, direct your statements to the student, not the coach.
- Provide the student with an opportunity to respond to comments and to disagree with you.
- Support and respect students as they share progress toward past goals, interests, skills, and limits.
- Consider the student an equal member of the IEP staffing team.

Teacher Roles

- Teach IEP meeting participation and leadership skills.
- Inform parents, administrators, and other team members when students are facilitating their own IEP meetings.

- Solicit support for the student from the IEP team.

- Support and coach the student through the IEP meeting.

- Teach students how to help attain IEP goals.

Administrator Roles

- Establish an environment that encourages active student involvement and leadership of the IEP process.

- Arrange for staff and parent training.

- Facilitate teaching of students' IEP skills prior to the student's attending the IEP meeting.

- Facilitate student's learning how to accomplish their IEP goals and objectives.

- Encourage infusion of self-determination concepts into other aspects of the school day.

Parent Roles

- Provide son or daughter the opportunity to learn crucial self-determination skills while they are still in a supportive educational environment.

- Discuss at home the student's progress in accomplishing goals.

- Discuss at home the student's interests, skills, and limits.

- Support the student's goals and the inevitable changes in the goals.

- If your vision of the future is different from your son's or daughter's, attempt to work out any differences before the meeting. If parents and students discuss these differences at the meeting it could give other team members the opportunity to impose their goals rather than those of the student or parent.

How Can Students Learn What Their Interests, Skills, and Limits Are Across the Different Transition Areas?

Aptitude measurement, work samples, interest inventories, and behavior checklists are being used in large numbers to assess skills and interests of individuals with disabilities (Agran & Morgan, 1991). Many educators appear to be using them to meet the IDEA requirement that goals and activities match student preferences and interests. Unfortunately, these assessment procedures often are methodologically flawed (Menchetti & Flynn, 1990). A single-point-in-time measurement approach is limited because the interests of individuals with disabilities often change with different experiences (Gaylord-Ross, 1986). An interest inventory completed on one day will not reflect changes in preferences gained through additional experience the next day (Buschner, Watts, Siders, & Leonard, 1989). Standardized assessments seldom help in the job placement process (Culver, Spencer, & Gliner, 1990). Verbal statements of job preferences often do not match the results from career interest inventories (Elrod, Sorgenfrei, & Gibson, 1989).

Some more helpful tools for developing student self-awareness that can be used as input to the transition planning process include self-directed situational assessment strategies using repeated measures and transition skills checklists that can be completed by the student, parent, or teacher. One variation on the transition skills checklist is the assessment included in the New Hats curriculum package (Curtis, 1996), which uses card decks composed of illustrations for students to show what their life is like now and what they would like to do in the future. More detailed information on assessment for transition can be found in Chapter 3 of this guide and in *Assess for Success* (Sitlington, Neubert, Begun, Lombard, & Leconte, 1996).

IMPLEMENTATION OF THE PLAN

What Must Students Do to Implement Their Plan?

Student participation in meetings is only the tip of the IEP iceberg. It is easy and fun to dream of possibilities, of what one would like to do in the future. It is another story, however, to make the dreams happen. Typically educators assume responsibility for accomplishing IEP goals. Rather than viewing goal attainment as the responsibility of the educator, consider for a moment a switch in this role. Educators need to teach students a generalizable process to attain their goals. At the same time, educators and parents need to support student's efforts in doing so.

Strategies that can be used to help students attain their goals are described in the following pargraphs. Although they were developed as part of specific curricula, they are described here to provide suggestions as to how teachers could use the goal attainment strategies specifically to help students assume leadership for achievement of their IEP goals, whether or not a particular curriculum is used. Detailed information about additional instructional strategies to support self-determination can be found in Chapter 4. Reviews of self-determination instructional materials are provided in Chapter 5.

Take Action (Martin, Huber-Marshall, Maxson, & Hughes, in press). A part of the *ChoiceMaker Self-Determination Curriculum*, this package teaches students a generalizable process to attain their IEP and personal goals. Central to the *Take Action* process is a series of questions that students answer to develop a plan, evaluate its effectiveness, and determine what changes are needed in order to reach their goals. To develop their plan students answer six questions:

1. Standard: What will I be satisfied with?

2. Feedback: How will I get information on my performance?

3. Motivation: Why do I want to do this?

4. Strategy: What methods should I use?

5. Support: What help do I need?

6. Schedule: When will I do it?

After evaluating whether or not each component of the plan helped them reach their goals, students answer the question: "What were the main reasons you got those results?"

Teachers may encourage students to use the *Take Action* process with all their IEP goals and other goals that are important in their lives. All student—not just those with IEPs—may use the strategies. Thus, teachers can use the process in general education academic and vocational environments, as well as in specialized learning situations.

Steps to Self-Determination (Field & Hoffman, 1996) This publication devotes 3 of the 16 lessons to helping students learn the steps needed to reach their short-term goals. First, students learn to use a stairstep process to break the major steps into doable smaller steps. Second, students learn to act on the steps needed to reach their goals by completing a sample goal exercise and homework. Third, students learn to overcome barriers to reaching their goals.

Take Charge for the Future (Powers, 1996b). This program includes a section on how to accomplish goals. Goal accomplishment is explained by saying "That means doing what you said you would do to work toward reaching your Dream. It also means helping people follow through on what they said they would do to help you" (p. 106). An emphasis is placed on helping students develop a problem-solving process to use in accomplishing their own goals and learning how to plan and secure support from others.

Whose Future Is It Anyway? (Wehmeyer & Kelchner, 1995). This package uses a process called "DO IT!" that consists of the following five steps: (1) define your problems, (2) outline your options, (3) identify the outcome of each option, (4) take action, and (5) get excited. By reading sample stories of youth dealing with real-life problems, students experience this process before they apply the process to their own lives.

Next S.T.E.P. (Halpern et al., 1997). After identifying crucial transition goals, this curriculum teaches students how to identify (a) specific activities and (b) resources needed to achieve goals. Students use individual guides to help them accomplish their goals.

What Are the Roles of Teachers, Administrators, and Parents in Implementing the Plan?

There is no better time than during the supportive school years to teach student self-determination skills, which include acting on as well as developing plans. After the school years are over, support structures outside the home are often difficult to obtain or do not exist at all. Therefore, the roles of teachers, administrators, and parents are crucial to the development of students' self-determination skills. Each player in this process must engage in unique roles to ensure success. Generalization of these skills will require overlearning and repeated practice in many different environments.

Teachers, administrators and parents can help in the following ways:

Teachers

- Teach IEP leadership and participation skills.
- Teach goal-attainment skills.
- Require and support the use of these skills to achieve IEP and non-IEP goals.
- Set up a system whereby students establish a plan and then report back regularly to show their results.
- Infuse self-determination skills into academic and vocational classes.

Administrators

- Establish an environment that encourages teachers to instruct students in self-determination skills.
- Encourage student leadership of the IEP process.
- Encourage teaching of student-directed goal-attainment strategies.
- Establish an environment that encourages and rewards students for using these skills to attain their IEP and other goals.

Parents

- Support student efforts to use self-determination skills to attain their goals while they are still in supportive school and home environments.

How Does Self-Determination Instruction Generalize to Being Successful in Adult Life?

Self-determined individuals know what they want, where they are going, how to get there, and when to make changes (see Chapter 1). Teaching self-determination skills while students are still in school is one way to help ensure success after students leave school. The IEP process is one of the few common opportunities students with disabilities across the country have to learn these important skills in a meaningful way.

For students to integrate these skills into their behavioral repertoire, they need repeated opportunities to practice their self-determination skills in pursuit of their self-chosen goals. The IEP, which includes both plan development and implementation, provides an excellent vehicle to help students acquire these skills while, at the same time, they are helping to develop meaningful educational and transition plans.

CONCLUSION

The time is now to teach students the skills needed for successful involvement in their IEP and transition process. It is a promising method to assist students to get involved and engaged in their education. Moreover, student participation and leadership of the IEP process is one way to begin teaching crucial self-determination skills, including self-awareness, decision making, goal attainment, self-evaluation, and adjustment. The IEP meeting is one of the most public aspects of the special education process. We can easily change it from being a bureaucratic administrative process into one that celebrates a student's education and places the student at the center of the educational process.

REFERENCES

Agran, M., & Morgan, R. L. (1991). Current transition assessment practices. *Research in Developmental Disabilities, 12*(2), 113–126. (ERIC Document Reproduction Service No. EJ 431 274)

Buschner, P. C., Watts, M. B., Siders, J. A., & Leonard, R. L. (1989). Career interest inventories: A need for analysis. *Career Development for Exceptional Individuals, 12*, 129–137. (ERIC Document Reproduction Service No. EJ 403 927)

Carpenter, W. D. (1995). *Become your own expert!* Minneapolis: Cognitive Learning Consultants.

Culver, J. B., Spencer, K. C., & Gliner, J. A. (1990). Prediction of supported employment placement by job developers. *Education and Training of the Mentally Retarded, 25*, 237–242. (ERIC Document Reproduction Service No. EJ 419 987)

Curtis, E. (1996). *Self-determination profile: An assessment package.* Salt Lake City: New Hats.

Elrod, G. F., Sorgenfrei, R. B., & Gibson, A. P. (1989). Agreement between the expressed and scales-determined career interests of adolescents with mild handicaps. *Career Development for Exceptional Individuals, 12*, 107–116. (ERIC Document Reproduction Service No. EJ 403 924)

Field, S., & Hoffman, A. (1996). *Steps to self-determination instructor's guide and student activity book.* Austin, TX: Pro-Ed.

Gaylord-Ross, R. (1986). The role of assessment in transitional, supported employment. *Career Development for Exceptional Individuals, 9*, 129–134. (ERIC Document Reproduction Service No. EJ 345 471)

Halpern, A. S., Herr, C. M., Wolf., N. K., Lawson, J. E., Doren, B., & Johnson, M. C. (1997). *Next S.T.E.P.: Student transition and educational planning.* Austin, TX: Pro-Ed.

Johnson, L. A., & Graham, S. (1990). Goal setting and its application with exceptional learners. *Preventing School Failure, 34*(4), 4–8.

Locke, E. A., Shaw, K. N., Saari, L. M., & Latham, G. P. (1981). Goal setting and task performance: 1969–1980. *Psychological Bulletin, 90*(1), 125–151.

Martin, J. E., & Huber Marshall, L. (1995). ChoiceMaker: A comprehensive self-determination transition program. *Intervention in School and Clinic, 30*, 147–156.

Martin, J. E., Huber Marshall, L., & Maxson, L. (1993). Transition policy: Infusing self-determination and self-advocacy into transition programs. *Career Development for Exceptional Individuals, 16*(1), 53–58.

Martin, J. E., Huber Marshall, L., Maxson, L., & Hughes, W. (in press). *Take action.* Longmont, CO: Sopris West.

Martin, J. E., Huber Marshall, L., Maxson, L., Jerman, P., & Miller, T. L. (1996). *The self-directed IEP.* Longmont, CO: Sopris West.

McGahee-Kovac, M. (1995). A student's guide to the IEP. *Washington, DC: National Information Center for Children and Youth with Disabilities.*

Menchetti, B. M., & Flynn, C. C. (1990). Vocational evaluation. In F. R. Rusch, (Ed.), *Supported employment: Models, methods, and issues* (pp. 111–130). Sycamore, IL: Sycamore.

Mithaug, D. E. (1996). Equal opportunity theory. Thousand Oaks, CA: Sage.

National Information Center for Children and Youth with Disabilities. (1995). Helping students develop their IEPs. Washington, DC: Author.

Powers, L. E. (1996a, June). *Promoting student involvement in transition planning: What does it take?* Presentation at the 11th annual Project Directors Meeting, Washington, DC.

Powers, L. (1996b). *Take charge for the future.* Portland: Child Development and Rehabilitation Center, Oregon Health Sciences University.

Sitlington, P. L., Neubert, D. A., Begun, W., Lombard, R. C., & Leconte, P. J. (1996). *Assess for success: Handbook on transition assessment.* Reston, VA: The Council for Exceptional Children.

Van Reusen, A. K., Bos, C. S., Schumaker, J. B., & Deshler, D. D. (1994). *The self-advocacy strategy.* Lawrence, KS: Edge Enterprises.

Ward, M. J., & Halloran, W. D. (1993). Transition issues for the 1990s. *OSERS News in Print, 6*(1), 4–5.

Wehmeyer, M., & Kelchner, K. (1995). *Whose future is it anyway?* Arlington, TX: The National ARC.

3

Assessment of Self-Determination

The purpose of this chapter is to

- Describe the link between self-determination and assessment.
- Identify the roles of students, educators, and family members related to assessment and self-determination.
- Provide techniques for assessing student traits and environmental characteristics related to self-determination.
- Discuss how assessment results can be used to promote self-determination.

What Is Assessment of Self-Determination?

Assessment and instruction are necessarily linked in all successful educational efforts, including self-determination. Assessment of self-determination involves (a) collecting information on factors that affect students' self-determination and (b) conducting all assessment in a manner that places students in a central role in the assessment process. According to Sitlington, Neubert, Begun, Lombard, and LeConte (1996), "assessment is integral to the self-determination process for all students with disabilities, even those with the most severe conditions" (p. 15).

Assessment of self-determination is important in two key ways:

1. Components of self-determination (e.g., student knowledge and skills, environmental factors) need to be assessed because they comprise an important instructional component of transition programming. Students who develop self-determination skills while in school are better able to self-assess and direct their career development in adulthood (Sitlington et al., 1996). Assessment of student and environmental characteristics related to self-determination is a key component of designing effective instructional programs to foster students' development of self-determination abilities.

2. Self-determination is an essential component of *all* successful assessment activities, across life skill and academic areas. Promoting self-determination through the assessment process helps ensure that (a) key points from the student's perspective are addressed in assessment and (b) the student has ownership in the assessment process and the subsequent educational planning efforts.

The purposes of assessment of self-determination will vary based on a number of factors. However, just as an emphasis on self-determination will change the way teaching proceeds (see Chapter 4), it will also change the way assessment is or should be done. These changes are driven by self-determination and empowerment, discussed in Chapter 1, and by the nature of instruction in self-determination. Assessment of self-determination shares features of both empowerment evaluation and the assessment of quality of life for people with disabilities.

Fetterman (1996) defined *empowerment evaluation* as "the use of evaluation concepts, techniques, and findings to foster improvement and self-determination" (p. 4). Although Fetterman's approach to empowerment evaluation has been addressed primarily to groups, some valuable contributions can be made by this evaluative approach to individual assessment. While traditional assessment orientations require that the assessor maintain impartiality and distance, this is not the case with empowerment evaluation. According to Fetterman (1996), "Empowerment evaluation has an unambiguous value orientation—it is designed to help people help themselves and improve their programs using a form of self-evaluation and reflection" (p. 5). Fetterman makes a critical point: An evaluator does not and cannot empower anyone; people empower themselves. Thus, one feature of assessment of self-determination must be that the student is an integral part of and equal partner in assessment activities. Assessment becomes a collaborative effort, combining the input of the student and other significant parties. Assessment includes an evaluation of the environment as well as the assessment of student characteristics.

Heal and Sigelman (1996) discussed methodological issues in quality-of-life measurement, and, to a large degree, these issues apply in the measurement of self-determination as well. These writers identified ways in which measurement methodologies can differ:

1. Measures can be objective (measuring the objective aspects of people's lives (e.g., employment status) or subjective (measuring attitudes and perceptions of the individual).

2. Measurement can directly index the characteristic to be measured (absolute measure) or use a relative index, such as comparison with some normative standard or ideal outcome.

3. Information about the characteristic being measured can be reported directly by the individual or by an outside observer.

These factors hold true for measuring self-determination. One can focus on objective measures such as whether individuals chose where they live or work or whether they engage in activities for which they have expressed a preference. A measure can also solicit subjective information such as attitudes or perceptions about control and competence in the student's life or other attitudinal components of self-determination. Self-determination is clearly a multidimensional construct, and assessment should include both subjective and objective measures.

What Is the Purpose of Assessment of Self-Determination in Education?

The primary use for assessment of self-determination is for instructional planning purposes. Students, their teachers, and their parents need to know what skills they have and what skills they need in order to become more self-determined. Within the context of empowerment evaluation, such activities must involve students as equal partners in the assessment process, which includes the decision-making process that emerges from assessment. Students can self-administer, score, and interpret assessments and work closely with teachers to identify curricular materials and noncurricular strategies to promote self-determination. Assessment has often been used to identify student weaknesses and to target instruction at those weaknesses. However, it is just as important to identify areas in which a student might excel and provide instruction or support to strengthen or reinforce skills in those areas as well as attempting to remediate areas of weakness.

A second important use of assessment of self-determination involves evaluation of student achievement. Assessment used for this purpose will provide information about student progress in acquiring skills related to self-determination. Again, it is important to include students in this process. Students can graph progress on assessments of individual skill areas or total self-determination and use this information to participate in decisions about continuing, terminating, or revising interventions.

A third use of assessment of self-determination is program evaluation. This type of assessment uses group data to evaluate programs, policies, and procedures. Assessment of self-determination can be used to evaluate teaching models or different environments and their impact on student self-determination. Additionally, information from self-determination assessment could be used in research related to self-determination, leading to new curricular strategies and further description of the characteristics of self-determination.

Who Conducts Self-Determination Assessment?

As mentioned earlier, self-determination assessment should be a team process. Just as high-quality transition planning requires input and commitment from persons with diverse perspectives, so does assessment of self-determination. Students, parents, teachers, and support services staff (e.g., counselors, psychologists, and adult service agency representatives) all play important roles in the self-determination assessment process.

The student is central in the assessment process, and he or she should participate in all assessment decisions, from what needs to be assessed to how it will be assessed to how the assessment results will be used. Students can also play an active role in collecting assessment data. This can include providing information about themselves as well as reporting information on ways in which their environments support or hinder self-determination. Parents and family members also are key participants in the self-determination assessment process. Parents have observed their son or daughter over a long period of time and often can provide a great deal of information about the student's strengths and weaknesses in areas related to self-determination. In addition, parents generally have the strongest emotional involvement with and attachment to the student. Their input in and ownership of the assessment process is critical.

Educators play a vital role in providing information, resources, and guidance to the assessment process. As with other aspects of self-determination, the teacher's role in the assessment process is primarily facilitative (e.g, providing support to the IEP team as they decide what needs to be assessed and how it will be assessed, coordinating administration of assessment instruments, and ensuring that assessment is used in a way that helps the student meet his or her goals).

The specific role that each individual (i.e., student, parent, teacher) will play depends on the needs and characteristics of the student, the relationship the individual has with the student, and environmental factors.

What Is the Role of the Student in Self-Determination Assessment?

The assessment process provides a vehicle to model, promote, and support self-determination. It is critical to the success of the overall assessment process that self-determination be supported as assessment is conducted. Students need to be active participants in deciding what needs to be assessed, how those factors will be measured, and how assessment results will be used. The student's role is at the center of the self-determination assessment process.

First, students should participate in determining the questions that need to be answered through assessment and help to design the assessment process that will be used. It is important that students understand and agree with the need for assessment and how assessment information will be obtained. Involving students at the beginning stages of the assessment process helps to ensure that key factors from the perspective of the student are addressed. It also creates ownership on the part of the student and helps him or her to continue to play an active role throughout the assessment process.

It is important that students be provided with the background information needed to participate in this decision-making process. Before the assessment process begins, students should be acquainted with the importance of and need for self-determination as well as some of the ways that self-determination can be measured. Students also need to understand the potential uses for assessment information.

Students can participate in the data-gathering phase of assessment in a number of ways. First, many self-determination assessments are self-report or interview instruments. The involvement of the student in this type of data gathering is obvious. Students also can help to assess opportunities for self-determination in their environments. Through using environmental checklists, students can help determine the supports and barriers to self-determination available to them in different settings.

Students also can seek involvement from people who are important to them in the self-determination process. For example, some self-determination assessment instruments measure perceptions of important people in students' lives (e.g, parents and teachers) about a student's level of self-determination. Students can request their participation and facilitate their inclusion in the assessment process.

Finally, students should be actively involved in using assessment data to plan and assess their progress in educational programs. This process was described in more detail in Chapter 2, "Student Involvement in Transition Planning." More information about specific self-determination assessment instruments can be found at the end of this chapter.

What Is the Role of Educators in Self-Determination Assessment?

A focus on empowerment evaluation redefines the role of educators in assessment. Zimmerman (cited in Fetterman, 1996) described the role of the professional in empowerment evaluation this way:

> An empowerment approach to intervention design, implementation, and evaluation redefines the professional's role relationship with the target population. The professional's role becomes one of collaborator and facilitator, rather than expert and counselor. The professional's skills, interests, or plans are not imposed on the community; rather, professionals become a resource for a community. (p. 5)

Just as the professional's role in empowerment evaluation, which is focused mainly on groups, is primarily facilitative, the educator's role in self-determination assessment for individual students is largely consultative and less directive. Educators can make four key contributions to the assessment process:

1. Knowledge of appropriate resources for assessment.

2. Technical skills in administering and interpreting assessment instruments and strategies.

3. Information about (a) educational and community resources and (b) community and employment expectations.

4. Interpersonal and group process skills that promote input from the various members of the transition team (i.e., students, parents, and adult service providers) when planning for, conducting, and using assessment.

An important role assumed by many educators related to assessment is that of service coordinator (Sitlington et al., 1996). Educators generally facilitate and coordinate the assessment effort. They often collect and review information from a variety of resources and facilitate the development of student portfolios and other documents to provide information for the educational planning team.

What Is the Role of the Family in Self-Determination Assessment?

Families and caregivers play a critical role in the development of self-determination, and school professionals need to work closely with them to promote appropriate family involvement in assessment. In establishing an effective team, the school professional recognizes that each team member brings unique expertise and capacity into play. Family members hold a wealth of information about students that cannot be gained otherwise. Additionally, family members are the only members of the educational planning and decision-making team, other than the student, who are involved with the student throughout his or her educational career.

Obtaining standardized information from family members (e.g., sending home surveys to be completed) can be useful, particularly if the same information is gathered from a variety of sources, including the student, his or her teacher, and others involved in the educational decision-making process. In addition to providing valuable information, this process can illuminate the diversity of perceptions or opinions about the student's capacity and current functioning and enable the team members to work toward a consensus.

Although it is helpful to collect standardized information from family members, a true partnership for assessment moves beyond simply sending a questionnaire home for a family member to complete. Soliciting input from family members can take several formats, from face-to-face open-context interviews to questionnaires and survey forms. Some specific ways in which family members can be involved in assessment that promotes self-determination include the following:

- Complete questionnaires and interviews.

- Provide information about observed student interests, preferences, and skills.

- Explore and help collect information on community recreational, residential, and employment options.

- Listen to students as they talk about their dreams, interests, goals, and needs.

- Support active student participation in assessment activities and educational planning meetings.

How Can Student Characteristics Related to Self-Determination Be Measured?

Several methods are available to assess student characteristics related to self-determination. According to Sitlington and colleagues (1996), adhering to the following principles helps to ensure appropriate assessment:

- Use a variety of methods to provide accurate assessment and verify assessment information.

- Use behavioral assessment as one of the key assessment methods.

- Use a collaborative approach to data collection and decision making.

This section provides an overview of methods that can be used to assess self-determination skills within the context of these principles. These methods include (a) analysis of background information, (b) interviews, (c) behavioral observation, (d) psychometric tests, and (e) curriculum-based assessment techniques.

Analysis of Background Information. One of the first available sources of information related to self-determination skills is material contained in the student's school records. These records may include previous assessments, individualized education programs, and observations of previous staff who have worked with the student. Records may also include information about previous student goals and reactions by students to specific community environments.

Student portfolio information may provide some of the most useful background information related to self-determination knowledge and skills. Students typically play a central role in assembling portfolio information, which is likely to be considered by the student as some of his or her best work.

By reviewing records, information about a student's preferences and interests as well as knowledge and skills may be gained. However, it is important to remember when reviewing previous records that (a) the information provided is from a previous point in time and may be more indicative of a student's history than his or her present level of functioning and (b) the information may be based on others' perceptions of the individual and may not be an accurate reflection of the student's self-perception.

Interviews. Interviews are used frequently in assessing student characteristics related to self-determination. Interviews provide an opportunity to gather information from a variety of important sources (e.g, the student, parents, other family members, friends, coworkers) about the student's self-determination skills, as well as his or her preferences, interests, goals, and past experiences. One of the greatest strengths of interviews is that they can help to identify needs as they are perceived by important individuals, including the student. They can also help to identify discrepancies in perception between important people in the student's life. For example, a student may state that his or her goal is to move into an apartment upon graduation from high school while the student's parents indicate that they expect that the transition to independent living will occur at a later time. It is important to identify these differences so they can be addressed. Understanding such differences can help the team (a) create the most accurate picture of the student's skills and desires, (b) develop the most appropriate transition goals, and (c) create a unified vision for the student and build a strong support base as he or she moves through the transition process.

Sitlington and colleagues (1996) listed seven steps to make the best use of the interview process. These steps are listed in Figure 3-1. Interview instruments available to assess self-determination are described at the end of this chapter.

Behavioral Observation. Behavioral observation is one of the best means available for evaluating many aspects of learning and development, but it is also one of the most abused assessment techniques (Schmidt, 1993). Observations provide an opportunity to assess applied skills in natural environments. However, they are also subject to the perceptual bias of the observer. The negative effect of perceptual bias can be limited by using a systematic procedure for observation and by having different persons observe the student in several different settings. Several systematic procedures for observing student behavior (i.e., narrative recording, time sampling, event sampling and rating scales) are described in *Assess for*

FIGURE 3-1
Steps in the interview Process

1. Come prepared with a set of specific questions.

2. Be flexible in following up on a specific question and obtaining clarifying or additional information. Always return, however, to your basic list of questions.

3. Conduct the interview in person, if possible, so that you can pick up on subtle cues from the person being interviewed, such as facial expressions and shifts in body posture.

4. Make the purpose of the interview clear and ensure the interviewee that there are no right or wrong answers.

5. Make the person as comfortable as possible. It may be a good idea to provide the person with a copy of the questions before the actual interview, especially if some of the questions require recall of specific facts or events from the past.

6. Write down enough information during the interview so you can remember the individual's responses. Take time right after the interview to complete your notes.

7. Try not to lead the person or insert your own personal biases or responses into the questions. Allow the person enough time to organize the answer before speaking. Also allow the person to respond as thoroughly as he or she chooses to a specific question.

Note. From *Assess for Success* by P. Sitlington, D. Neubert, W. Begun, R. Lombard, & P. Leconte, 1996. Copyright © The Council for Exceptional Children. Reprinted with permission.

Success by Sitlington and colleagues (1996). Behavioral checklists to systematically record behaviors associated with self-determination are described at the end of this chapter.

Psychometric Tests*.* Psychometric tests are formal paper-and-pencil standardized instruments. They are administered and scored using uniform procedures. They have generally been field tested with sample groups. Psychometric tests can be either norm referenced or criterion referenced. *Norm-referenced* tests compare an individual student's performance to the performance of a group, and *criterion-referenced* instruments compare a student's performance to a set of specific standards or learning objectives.

Standardized instruments can be used to compare (a) student performance over time, (b) a student's performance with the performance of other students, or (c) a student's performance against specific standards. The primary use of standardized instruments in self-determination is to compare student performance over time and to evaluate the effectiveness of a self-determination instructional program. There is little benefit, and potentially great harm, to comparing a student's self-determination to that of other students.

As stated previously, it is very important to use a variety of assessment methods to obtain an accurate picture of a student's skills and instructional needs. This is especially important when using standardized tests. Standardized tests do not measure a student's ability to use skills in real settings. In addition, they may provide misleading results if the student doesn't understand the questions provided in the testing format or has text anxiety. However, as part of a complete assessment approach, standardized instruments can be useful in assessing self-determination skills by providing a standard or scale against which student characteristics can be measured. As with any assessment strategy, the value of a standardized instrument will be determined by how the results are used to create a positive difference in the student's life.

A variety of standardized instruments have been developed to assess self-determination knowledge and skills. These instruments are described at the end of this chapter.

Curriculum-Based Assessment Techniques*.* Curriculum-based assessment techniques, including portfolio assessment, are increasingly being used in general and special education. Curriculum-based assessment refers to assessment based on what students are taught within a curriculum. There are eight steps in curriculum-based assessment (Salvia & Hughes, 1990):

1. State the purpose for the assessment.
2. Analyze the curriculum.
3. Develop behavioral objectives.
4. Design assessment procedures.

5. Collect data.

6. Summarize the data.

7. Display the data.

8. Interpret the data and make decisions.

One curriculum-based assessment approach that is consistent with self-determination is portfolio assessment. Portfolios provide an opportunity for students to assemble materials that document their progress in a given area. Students help define the criteria against which their work will be judged. They then assess and present samples of their work to demonstrate their performance and progress in that area. Portfolio assessment is a move toward more authentic assessment, allowing student progress in real settings to be examined. To effectively implement a portfolio assessment process, students must be actively involved throughout the process (Keefe, 1995).

While it is possible to use many different formats for presentation of portfolio materials, portfolios are usually contained in some type of folder or notebook. Many districts have also begun to use electronic portfolios, with students maintaining documentation of their accomplishments on a computer disc. An introduction is written to describe the content area and define performance objectives or assessment criteria. Materials that demonstrate performance related to the area are then provided. A wide variety of materials may be used to document student performance, including informal assessments, interest inventories, writing samples, summaries of teacher observations, records of reading, work samples, photographs, videos, and tape recordings.

Just as portfolios provide an assessment process that can promote self-determination across content areas, they can also be an effective tool for assessing and recording self-determination skills. For example, a young woman who was involved in a curriculum to promote self-determination skills used a portfolio to document her progress in developing skills that would lead to greater self-determination. In her portfolio she documented progress toward meeting a goal she had established. Her goal was to obtain her driver's license. She documented her performance on required tests for the license as well as keeping a journal about the skills she was developing and the feelings she had as she worked to achieve her goal. The portfolio provided an excellent tool that helped her assess and demonstrate her progress toward her goal and identify skills she needed to develop further.

How Can Environmental and Contextual Characteristics Related to Self-Determination Be Assessed?

As discussed in Chapter 4, the environment plays a critical role in the development of self-determination. If the physical environment is not conducive to promoting student choice, students will not have the opportunity to apply their skills and engage in the experiences that lead to becoming self-determined. Environmental characteristics include all contextual factors that enhance or impede choice, decision making, and student control. These factors include social and cultural aspects of the environment (e.g., school and classroom rules, school climate) as well as aspects of the physical environment (e.g., architectural barriers, classroom seating arrangements). Environmental factors can be classroom based or school-wide characteristics.

Assessment needs to focus on the total environment, including both the opportunities afforded to students to become self-determined and the physical aspects of the environment. Physical features of the environment that are important to evaluate are discussed in Chapter 4. Beyond the fact that environments need to be accessible to students using wheelchairs or other mobility devices, the physical layout of the classroom—including placement of tables, equipment, and learning materials—should increase the potential that students will plan, initiate, and direct their own activities. There should be a variety of stimulus materials readily available, and there should be time scheduled for students to access these materials. Environments that are too noisy or overcrowded will limit exploration and initiation. Students should view the environment as "their" place. In addition to these open spaces, students should have a place within the environment that they control or "own," such as their desk area. Cook, Brotherson, Weigel-Garrey, and Mize (1996) provided an example of an assessment that examines these factors in an environment, in this case a student's home environment.

Wolman, Campeau, DuBois, Mithaug, and Stolarski (1994) developed a scale that evaluates students' opportunities to identify and express their own interests, set expectations and goals, make choices and plans to meet goals, take actions to complete plans, evaluate the results of their actions, and alter plans and actions. (This assessment instrument is further described in the final section of this chapter.) Such opportunities can be limited by teacher control orientation, classroom or campus rules and regulations, the expectations of others about the students, and the students' perceptions about themselves. Environmental assessment should take into account all of these factors.

What Resources are Available to Assess Self-Determination?

In 1992, the U.S. Department of Education, Office of Special Education and Rehabilitative Services (OSERS) established a priority to develop conceptual models and assessment approaches for self-determination for students with disabilities. In addition, some assessment instruments were developed through the OSERS-funded self-determination model demonstration projects. Brief descriptions of the assessment approaches and instruments developed through these projects follows.

AIR Self-Determination Scale and User Guide. The main purpose of the AIR Self-Determination Scale and User Guide (Wolman et al., 1994) is to "provide an easy-to-use tool to assess and develop strategies for improving a student's level of self-determination" (p. 9). The scale was designed to be used with all school-age students, grades K through 12+. It can be used to (a) assess and develop a profile of a student's level of self-determination, (b) determine strengths and areas for improvement to increase self-determination, (c) identify goals and objectives, and (d) develop strategies to increase a student's capacities and opportunities. The scale measures *capacity* (i.e., ability, knowledge, and perceptions) and *opportunity* (at school and at home) related to three components of self-determination: *thinking, doing, and adjusting.* A five-point Likert-type scale (1 = never; 5 = always) is used to rate students and environments on self-determination components. There are three forms of the scale. The educator form is intended for use by teachers. The student form can be used by students who have the requisite reading and comprehension skills. The parent form is intended for use with parents who could benefit by considering the self-determination of their sons or daughters. The forms were field-tested with students between the ages of 6 and 25. Further information about the AIR Self-Determination Scale can be obtained from American Institutes for Research, P.O. Box 1113, Palo Alto, CA 94302. Telephone: 415/493-3550.

The Arc's Self-Determination Scale. The Arc's Self-Determination Scale (Wehmeyer, 1995) is a student self-report measure of self-determination designed for use by adolescents with disabilities, particularly students with mild cognitive and learning disabilities. The 72-item scale measures overall self-determination and the domain areas of autonomy, self-regulation, psychological empowerment, and self-realization. The scale includes four-point Likert-type scale items, story completion items (i.e., the beginning and ending of a story are provided and the student writes the middle section), items that require the student to identify goals and break the goals into smaller steps, and items that require students to make a choice between two options. The scale can be completed by the student independently or it can be read to the student. The scale can be administered to 15 students at one time, provided students' reading abilities warrant this and there are enough persons to provide necessary support to students during scale administration. For further information on The Arc's Self-Determination Scale contact The Arc of the United States, 500 East Border Street, Suite 300, Arlington, TX 76010. Telephone: 817/261-6003. This scale may also be ordered from The Council for Exceptional Children, 1920 Association Drive, Reston, VA 20191-1589. Telephone: 888/232-7323.

ChoiceMaker Self-Determination Assessment. The ChoiceMaker Self-Determination Assessment (Martin & Marshall, 1996) is a curriculum-based assessment and planning tool intended for use with middle to high school students with emotional or behavior disabilities and mild to moderate learning problems. It may be adapted for older elementary students or for students with more severe learning problems. The ChoiceMaker assessment measures student skills and opportunities at school in three areas: choosing goals, expressing goals, and taking action. The assessment has three parts. The first part is a rating scale of student skills related to self-determination and opportunities at school to perform each of the self-determination-related skills. Student skills and opportunities are rated on a scale from 0 to 4. The second part of the assessment is an assessment profile. The student skills and school opportunities ratings are recorded on a profile where differences in scores are more readily apparent. The third part of the assessment, the ChoiceMaker Curriculum Matrix, provides objectives and corresponding goals for consideration as teaching priorities. Further information on the ChoiceMaker Self-Determination Assessment can be obtained from Sopris West Publishers, 1140 Boston Avenue, Longmont, CO 80501. Telephone: 800/547-6747.

The Self-Determination Assessment Battery. The Self-Determination Assessment Battery (Hoffman, Field, & Sawilowsky, 1995) measures cognitive, affective, and behavioral factors related to self-determination. These factors are assessed from the perspectives of the student, teacher, and parent. The battery is based on the Field and Hoffman model of self-determination. The model focuses on those variables related to self-determination that are within the individual's control and are potential targets for instructional intervention. The model contains five components: Know Yourself, Value Yourself, Plan, Act, and Experience Outcomes and Learn. There are five instruments in the battery. The Self-Determination Knowledge Scale (forms A and B) (Hoffman, Field, & Sawilowsky, 1996) is a multiple-choice and true/false format instrument designed to assess students' cognitive knowledge of self-determination skills as taught in the *Steps to Self-Determination* (Field & Hoffman, 1996) curriculum. The Self-Determination Observation Checklist is a 38-item behavioral checklist designed to be used by classroom teachers. Students are observed over a class period, and behaviors that have been found to be correlated with self-determination are checked. The Self-Determination Student Scale is a 92-item self-report instrument completed by the student that measures both affective and cognitive aspects of self-determination. The items contain a brief stimulus, to which the student marks "That's me" or "That's not me." The Teacher Perception Scale and the Parent Perception Scale are 30-item questionnaires on which teachers or parents rate their student or child on a five-point Likert-type scale on a variety of behaviors, abilities, and skills associated with self-determination. The instruments in the battery can be used separately or together to assess student variables associated with self-determination. Further information about the Self-Determination Knowledge Scale can be obtained from Pro-Ed, 8700 Shoal Creek Boulevard, Austin, TX 78757-6897. Telephone: 512/451-3246. It is also available from The Council for Exceptional Children. Telephone: 888/232-7733. Information about the Self-Determination Assessment Battery is available from the Self-Determination and Transition Projects Office, 469 Education Building, College of Education, Wayne State University, Detroit, MI 48202. Telephone: 313/577-1638.

The Self-Determination Profile: An Assessment Package. This package (Curtis, 1996) is one of the New Hats curriculum sets designed to help youth and adults determine their preferences, activities, relationships and routines as they are now as well as into the future. Students use card decks composed of illustrations to show what their life is now like and what they would like to do in the future. Various summary sheets are provided for student use, along with facilitator instructions. The Self-Determination Profile: An Assessment Package is available from New Hats, Inc., P.O. Box 57567, Salt Lake City, UT 84157. Telephone: 801/268-9811.

How Should Results from Self-Determination Assessment Be Used?

The way in which assessment is used determines whether the assessment process is helpful or harmful to the student. Assessment results that are misused (i.e., that do not lead to improvement of the educational program or to greater quality of life) are detrimental to the student and are likely to result in more negative consequences than would occur if assessment were not conducted. On the other hand, assessment that is used appropriately can make a positive difference in students' lives. For example, at a recent self-determination meeting, a high school junior with a learning disability spoke eloquently and positively about a standardized test that he felt changed his life. When his learning disability was diagnosed through an assessment process using standardized instruments, the information was used to help him understand why he was having difficulty in school and to put in place necessary accommodations. The assessment was valuable *because the information was used to make a positive difference in his life.* Assessment has value only if the results are used properly. It is critical that the process used to assess self-determination promote self-determination. Students need to be involved in reviewing and using assessment information.

There are four primary uses for self-determination assessment results:

1. Promoting self-awareness.
2. Instructional planning.
3. Making accommodations and creating opportunities in the environment.
4. Program evaluation.

Promoting Self-Awareness. As discussed in Chapter 1, an awareness of one's needs, interests and preferences, skills, and limitations, is a fundamental component of self-determination. Results of self-determination assessment can be used to help individuals develop more accurate pictures of themselves and their current environments. This awareness can be used to help students decide what is most important to them and develop greater self-acceptance and confidence. For assessment information to be most valuable in promoting self-awareness it is important that

• Students' strengths be identified and emphasized, as well as areas for improvement.

• Assessment results be explained in the context of real, applied situations.

- Environmental factors influencing self-determination, including supports and barriers, be identified, as well as student characteristics.
- The student be provided with the opportunity to reflect and comment on assessment results.

Instructional Planning. One of the most important uses of assessment of self-determination skills is for instructional planning. By developing a picture of a student's current skill levels, the educational team can make decisions about the student's needs and the most appropriate use of the student's instructional time. For assessment to be used for instructional planning, assessment procedures must be carefully chosen so that information that is useful for planning is provided. For example, if a standardized test is given that measures self-determination skills but does not yield information about specific areas of strength and weakness, the instrument will likely yield little information that is useful for specific educational planning. However, a curriculum-based assessment process designed around an instructional program available in the school would likely yield valuable information for educational planning. In addition to selecting appropriate instruments and strategies, assessment results need to be reviewed, understood, and used by the members of the educational team, including the student, with an eye to designing the most appropriate instruction.

Making Accommodations in the Environment. Self-determination is affected by both environmental supports and barriers and the knowledge, skills, and beliefs of the individual. Environmental assessment may reveal that there are few opportunities to practice self-determined behaviors in the student's environment, or that there are other substantial barriers to self-determination, such as a punitive, overly controlling authority figure or a lack of order and predictable consequences. If self-determination is to be maximized, it is important that assessment results be used to create changes in the environment as well as in the skill levels of the student.

Student Progress and Program Evaluation. Assessment results also can be used to monitor student progress and evaluate instructional programs. Information gleaned by comparing a student's performance prior to and after instruction can be used to assess student progress and also to determine new instructional goals. Assessment results can determine the effectiveness of instructional programs and be used to make program modifications. Standardized instruments, criterion or norm referenced, are most often used for this evaluative purpose because they provide a consistent standard against which progress can be measured. However, the use of more authentic techniques, such as systematic observation, curriculum-based assessment, and portfolio assessment, should not be overlooked for this purpose. By examining themes in various assessment results, valuable information for measuring student progress and program effectiveness can be obtained.

CONCLUSION

Assessment is an important component in the development of self-determination in students. As in any instructional program, assessment is an important first step to designing effective instruction. Furthermore, the way in which assessment is used across content areas affects student self-determination. Students need to play a central role in the assessment process, including determining the purpose of assessment, designing the assessment process, collecting and interpreting data, and using assessment results for planning and evaluation. Parents, teachers, and support services specialists (e.g, psychologists, counselors, and social workers) also play important roles in self-determination assessment. Through both the process and outcomes of a team orientation to assessment, student self-determination can be fostered.

REFERENCES

Cook, C. C., Brotherson, M. J., Weigel-Garrey, C., & Mize, I. (1996). Homes to support the self-determination of children. In D. J. Sands & M. L. Wehmeyer (Eds.), *Self-determination across the life span: Independence and choice for people with disabilities*, (pp. 89–108). Baltimore: Paul H. Brookes.

Curtis, E. (1996). Self-determination Profile: An assessment package. Salt Lake City: New Hats.

Fetterman, D. M. (1996). Empowerment evaluation: An introduction to theory and practice. In D. M. Fetterman, S. J. Kaftarian, & A. Wandersman (Eds.), *Empowerment evaluation: Knowledge and tools for self-assessment and accountability*, (pp. 3–46). Thousand Oaks, CA: Sage.

Field, S., & Hoffman, A. (1996). *Steps to self-determination*. Austin, TX: Pro-Ed.

Heal, L. W., & Sigelman, C. K. (1996). Methodological issues in quality of life measurement. In R. L. Schalock (Ed.), *Quality of life: Conceptualization and measurement* (pp. 91–104). Washington, DC: American Association on Mental Retardation.

Hoffman, A., Field, S., & Sawilowksy, S. (1995). *Self-determination assessment battery user's guide*. Detroit, MI: Wayne State University.

Hoffman, A., Field, S., & Sawilowsky, S. (1996). Self-Determination Knowledge Scale (forms A and B). Austin, TX: Pro-Ed.

Keefe, C. H. (1995). Portfolios: Mirrors of learning. *TEACHING Exceptional Children, 27*, 66–67. (ERIC Document Reproduction Service No. EJ 494 807)

Martin, J., & Marshall, L. (1996). ChoiceMaker Self-Determination Assessment. Colorado Springs: University of Colorado.

Salvia, J., & Hughes, C. (1990). *Curriculum-based assessment: Testing what is taught.* New York: Macmillan.

Schmidt, J. J. (1993). *Counseling in schools: Essential services and comprehensive programs.* Needham Heights, MA.: Allyn and Bacon.

Sitlington, P. L., Neubert, D., Begun, W., Lombard, R., & LeConte, P. (1996). *Assess for success.* Reston, VA: The Council for Exceptional Children.

Wehmeyer, M. (1995). The Arc's Self-Determination Scale. Arlington, TX: The Arc of the United States.

Wolman, J. M., Campeau, P. L., DuBois, P. A., Mithaug, D.E., & Stolarski V. S. (1994). AIR Self-Determination Scale and User Guide. Palo Alto, CA: American Institutes for Research.

4

Instructional Practices that Promote Self-Determination

The purpose of this chapter is to

- Identify specific curricular practices, topics, and strategies to be addressed at both the elementary and secondary levels to promote self-determination and self-advocacy.

- Suggest family roles in promoting self-determination for students.

- Describe roles of school administrators in promoting self-determination for students.

- Discuss noncurricular and environmental considerations for teachers in establishing self-determination in the classroom.

Why Do We Need to Spend Instructional Time Teaching Knowledge and Skills for Self-Determination?

There is little doubt that educators, parents, politicians, business people, and the general public are concerned with the state of education in the nation's elementary and secondary schools. There is considerable evidence that students of all abilities often leave high school without the skills they need to be successful in adult life. For all young people, the skills and abilities they hold at the time of their transition to adult life are considered a measure of the success of the educational system. To this end, many follow-up studies have been conducted to examine educational outcomes for youth with disabilities. These studies have confirmed that many students with disabilities are making the transition to adult life without the skills required to be successful members of society. Too few people with disabilities live independently, are competitively employed in a full-time capacity, or are employed at a living wage (e.g., Hasazi, Gordon, & Roe, 1985; Siegel, Robert, Waxman, & Gaylord-Ross, 1992; Sitlington, Frank, & Carson, 1992). Likewise, too few people with disabilities continue in postsecondary education to learn the employment skills needed for the 21st century (Fairweather

& Shaver, 1991; Wagner et al., 1991). Disability status has been found to have a strong, consistent, and negative influence on occupational aspirations of high school seniors (Rojewski, 1996). The cumulative results of these studies have spurred a reexamination of the efficacy of special education.

One of the significant changes brought about by this reexamination is a commitment by many special educators to focus on educational outcomes that will assist students to become self-determined—to develop the skills they need to take charge of their own educational programs, meet their own educational goals, and prepare for their lives after graduation. Such focus has its historical roots in the career development movement. Super (1983) identified a set of attitudinal and cognitive factors important to career development. Attitudinal factors that represent the readiness to make career choices and focus on career goals include the following:

• The ability to plan for near and distant futures.

• The ability to take control of one's own life (locus of control).

• An understanding of the relationship of time to goal attainment.

• Healthy self-esteem.

• The ability and willingness to explore careers and opportunities.

• The willingness to ask questions and seek solutions.

• The willingness to seek out and use resources.

• The willingness to participate in school-based and community-based activities.

Cognitive factors identified by Super (1983) as important in career development include (a) information for decision making, (b) decision-making skills, (c) self-knowledge, (d) work experience, (e) crystallization of personal values and interests, and (f) preferences in occupations. Using these skills, young adults can develop a realistic vision of their strengths and limitations and a reality orientation that assists them to identify their needs, wants, and aspirations and to focus their efforts to attain appropriate goals.

Many students with disabilities have encountered difficulties developing these important skills and attitudes. In a review of literature, Biller (1985) found that students with disabilities often:

• Exhibit an external locus of control.

• Exhibit low self-esteem.

• Exhibit poor planning and goal-setting skills.

• Participate least in extracurricular activities.

• Have difficulty in gathering information for decision making.

• Are weak in career decidedness at the time of graduation.

• Have a weak reality orientation regarding their strengths and limitations and the relationship of that self-knowledge to career choice.

The cumulative effect of these characteristics is that adolescents with disabilities are often less able to make career decisions and are less prepared for adult responsibilities than their nondisabled peers. Students with disabilities are often unable to advocate for their own needs, wants, and desires and less prepared to make the hard choices and decisions needed to take control of their own lives and become self-determined adults (e.g., Wehmeyer, 1993; Wehmeyer & Kelchner, 1994). Learned helplessness and self-deprecating attributions have been widely documented among students with learning disabilities (Smith, 1989) and also present barriers to student self-determination (Field, 1996).

This information confirms that students with disabilities are not learning the skills related to career development and self-determination on an informal basis and that these skills and attitudes must be structured into the school curriculum. Furthermore, there is growing evidence of a causal link between the skills of self-determination and positive adult outcomes. In a study conducted by The Arc, Wehmeyer and Schwartz (1996) found that 1 year after graduation, students with learning disabilities or mental disabilities who were self-determined were more likely to have achieved more positive adult outcomes, including being employed at a higher rate and earning more per hour when compared to peers who were not self-determined. Reexamination and refocusing to address these important educational issues must occur so that more students will attain desired outcomes. Education is, after all, first and foremost preparation of the learner for success in life.

How Does Teaching Self-Determination Change the Curriculum?

A fundamental shift in focus is occurring in special education. Rather than continue to rely upon an instructional model in which the teacher is given full responsibility for determining when, why, what, where, and how a student will learn, we are beginning to realize that there may be marked advantages in involving the student more actively in educational decision making as well as the delivery of instruction itself (Agran, 1997).

Teaching self-determination will have profound effects on both the classroom curriculum and the school curriculum. Teaching self-determination means a student-centered focus. It requires teaching more process and problem-solving skills. It means spending more curricular time enabling students to learn about themselves. Promoting self-determination requires that education become student directed. In high school, this means that students need to choose their courses and make choices based on their plans for the future. Students can only make such plans for the future if they have explored their strengths and limitations and examined the options available to them. Students need to be actively involved in making career decisions. Will they take a college prep, tech prep, or general curriculum? They need to understand that the choices they make will have effects on their opportunities and options in the future. Every choice one makes has an "opportunity cost." If a student chooses not to take algebra, this decision will have effects on his or her ability to go to a 4-year college. Students should be enabled to understand the potential opportunity and the potential cost. If curricular choices are made without the participation of the student, then why should the student develop ownership of the 4-year plan? Why should students be motivated to work toward plans that do not represent their needs, wants, and aspirations?

Self-determination is both a focal point for instruction and an umbrella under which curricular decisions are made. Promoting self-determination means assisting students to explore alternative choices, examine the consequences of each choice, make decisions, and learn from the consequences of the choices that were made. Such a focus is a significant move away from making choices for students in favor of teaching students to make choices and solve problems for themselves. As an analogy, self-determination means teaching the student to drive the car, not ride in the back seat. Like the job of people who are teaching adolescents to drive, the job of educators is to make sure they have the entry-level skills and then pray that they are not injured in their first solo attempt. This means that choice making, decision making, and problem solving are longitudinal issues in the curriculum. Children must be taught the skills leading to self-determination throughout their school experiences, from elementary through high school. Practice in goal setting and choice making is a must if we are to feel confident that the student can "drive the car" after passing the initial driver's test.

Self-directed learning is a key to achieving self-determination and has profound ramifications for changing the curriculum. Educators must learn to allow students to make choices even if these are not the choices that we would make. We cannot empower students if we do not allow such opportunities. In order to maximize the likelihood that students will make good decisions, we must provide practice across the curriculum in decision making as well as extensive opportunities to develop knowledge of personal strengths and limitations.

One of the primary goals for educators will be to develop a curricular safety net to make sure that the consequences of choice making and decision making are not dangerous or extreme and that there is always an alternative to choices A, B, and C after the initial attempt to be self-determined. There should always be a way back from mistakes in decision making. Failure is only a learning experience when it is followed by success. Self-observation, self-evaluation, and self-reinforcement are all skills that will need to be taught in this new curriculum model. The goal of this new curriculum model is to develop goal-oriented learners who are active, involved, engaged, motivated, interested, excited, and focused on the prize. The prize is a student vision of who he or she is and who he or she is going to become. The prize is a student with the skills of self-determination.

What Are Some Specific Curricular Practices and Topics to Be Addressed for Elementary-Age Students?

The development of characteristics related to self-determination was described in Chapter 1, including a brief summary of instructional efforts tied to development. It is obvious from that description that it is important to address self-determination before students enter middle and high school. Intervention at both elementary and secondary levels will necessarily involve curriculum-based practices and noncurricular strategies. (The latter will be addressed later in this chapter.) In this guide, the distinction between curricular and noncurricular is meant to represent the difference between *what* we teach and *how* we teach (Sands, Adams, & Stout, 1995). Curricular strategies refer to what we should teach to promote self-determination; noncurricular strategies indicate how we should teach, including methodological and environmental concerns. In practice, there is much overlap between these, but the dichotomy is useful for purposes of illustration.

During the elementary years, the most important factor contributing to the development and acquisition of self-determination is that instructional efforts include opportunities for students to make choices about all aspects of learning. Abery and Zajac (1996) suggested that instead of having young children engaged in preselected skill-building activities, educational activities should be child directed, allowing frequent opportunities for choice throughout the instructional day. Brown, Appel, Corsi, and Wenig (1993) listed seven ways to infuse choices into instructional activities. These include

1. Choosing within an activity.

2. Choosing between two or more activities.

3. Deciding when to do an activity.

4. Selecting the person with whom to participate in an activity.

5. Deciding where to do an activity.

6. Refusing to participate in a planned activity.

7. Choosing to end an activity at a self-selected time (Gothelf & Brown, 1996, p. 362).

Some children with more significant disabilities may need instruction on how to make choices, including how to communicate preferences and select from options (Reid, Parsons, & Green, 1991). Choice-making experiences become the building blocks to promote other aspects of self-determination, such as self-regulation, decision making, and problem solving. For example, children can be encouraged to *reconsider* choices they have made, evaluate outcomes from those choices, and consider alternative options they could have selected, thereby learning basic elements of problem-solving and decision-making skills. Generally, younger children need to have more opportunities to think through problems, choices, and decisions aloud. Although they are not ready to make decisions independently or solve problems, they can learn by talking through these processes with adults. During the late elementary years, this can become more systematic. Doll, Sands, Wehmeyer, and Palmer (1996) suggested having students write a problem at the top of a sheet of paper, list all possible choices they can generate, and identify the benefits and costs of each choice.

During the late elementary years students can begin to learn more about goal-oriented behavior. Teachers can work with students to generate personal or academic goals. The students in turn can write down their goals; monitor their performance on objectives associated with the goals by graphing, recording, or otherwise charting performance or behavior; and evaluate their progress. One strategy that can be useful for social and behavioral goals is the use of contracts with students. These can be student generated or developed by the teacher, but they should provide students with a clear description of the steps they must achieve to reach a specific goal and the benefits from achieving that goal.

Many of the activities important to self-awareness, including the identification of preferences and interests, should begin in the elementary years. Younger children can be encouraged to think and talk about how they learn, what they do well, and what they like the most. Older elementary-age children can begin to think more about where they have weaknesses in key skill areas, although the emphasis should remain on what students do well. It should go without saying that such efforts must be supportive and focused on enabling the student to discover his or her strengths and limitations. Any focus on limitations must be coupled with supports for students to accommodate or compensate for limitations and framed within an approach that celebrates students' uniqueness.

Shure (1992) identified several cognitive skills that are important to the development of effective problem-solving skills. The development of perspective taking, as discussed earlier, is an important marker of the emergence of problem-solving skills. Children should be provided opportunities to identify others' thoughts and feelings and learn to take into account other people's points of view. Involving students in brainstorming sessions is a good way to foster the generation of multiple options and solutions to problems.

It is not too early to begin to focus on self-advocacy skills during the elementary years. Younger students should be provided opportunities to learn the difference between anger and assertiveness. Older students can practice, through role modeling and scripting, situations in which being assertive is appropriate. It is also useful to introduce students to different types of communication—verbal and nonverbal—and provide them with opportunities to develop basic leadership and team skills.

What Are Some Specific Curricular Strategies to Promote Self-Determination for Secondary-Age Students?

A CASE STUDY

Jason was a 17-year-old junior in high school with a learning disability. In the summer of 1994, he was participating in summer school for two reasons. First, he needed to make up educational credits for courses that he had not passed during the academic year. Second, participation in summer school in the morning was required so he could participate in his paid summer job in the afternoon. When Jason began his morning summer math class he sat apart from the other eight young adults in the class and seemed to be uninterested in what the group was learning. When asked to participate, Jason let the instructor know that what was being taught was of no interest to him because he was going to join the Army.

Whether during the summer or during the academic year, this scenario occurs far too often. Students who seem uninterested, unmotivated, and disengaged from the curriculum and educational activities are far too common. In this case, however, the instructor was prepared to use some specific best-practice strategies based in the self-determination literature to work with Jason. First, the instructor told Jason that he was thrilled that Jason had a goal for life after high school and that a career in the military was a fine choice. Second, the instructor asked Jason what he wanted to do in the Army. Jason told the instructor that he wanted to work in electronic repair and that what the other students were learning in mathematics was unimportant and a waste of his time. Next, the instructor asked Jason if he had ever taken the Armed Services Vocational Aptitude Battery (ASVAB) or talked to an Army recruiter. He pointed out to Jason that in order to get into the Army he would have to take the ASVAB and obtain a predetermined score on a portion of the test called the Armed Forces Qualifying Test (AFQT). Just wanting to get into the service was not enough. Only those persons who did well on the test would be admitted into the Army. The instructor also told him that if he passed the AFQT the other scores on the ASVAB would determine whether he would qualify for the field of electronic repair.

Over the next several days, the instructor and Jason worked out a plan of study for his morning summer school experience. First, with his parents' permission, Jason would make an appointment with the local Army recruiter. Jason would independently go to the recruiting station and find out more about the ASVAB test and other requirements for joining the Army. Jason and the English instructor would design a series of questions that Jason would ask about joining the armed forces, and Jason agreed to write a report based on the answers to his questions. This question-asking technique was identified as important by the instructor to assist Jason in developing problem-solving skills for decision making.

While at the recruiting station, Jason would sign up to take the ASVAB test. Jason was given a pass to be signed by the recruiter to confirm that he had met his obligation and attended his appointment at the predetermined time. The math instructor found curriculum material that Jason agreed was important to him. At the local bookstore, the instructor purchased a workbook that focused on preparing to take the ASVAB test. This workbook included sample ASVAB questions in all areas of the test including applied mathematics, problem solving, and math for electronics. During mathematics class, Jason agreed to take specific ASVAB tests. The instructor and Jason corrected the timed tests and discussed Jason's strengths and weaknesses in each area of the tests. The instructor offered to work with Jason to improve his math skills in the areas that Jason and the instructor found to be deficient. The instructor also agreed to provide independent seatwork for Jason so he could practice the skills he had decided he needed to improve to meet his goals. Since meeting the criteria of mathematics required by the Army on the AFQT was important to Jason, he worked extremely hard during math class for the remainder of summer school because he was working toward his personal life goals. Jason was engaged, self-motivated, and focused on the curriculum. The curriculum was focused on his goals and aspirations.

This scenario actually occurred, and it represents the power of self-determination for improving educational outcomes. Like too many young adults, Jason viewed the existing curriculum as uninteresting and lacking relevance to his life. Once that relevance was established, Jason became motivated to work toward his goals. Several best-practice strategies were included in this example; they are discussed in greater detail in the following paragraphs.

Students need *practice identifying both long- and short-term goals*. In the previous scenario, Jason's long-term goal was to enlist in the military. What incremental steps can the teacher plan to help him work toward his goal while he is in high school? How can we assist him to reach toward his goal and explore other options along the way? For example, perhaps there are other careers that Jason could explore in the military. What if he does not pass the ASVAB test at the criteria for entrance? He may choose to retake the test on several more occasions over his time in high school. Will he choose to explore careers outside the military? Will he decide, based on the experience of taking the test, that he can or cannot pass the test? An important role for Jason's teacher was to applaud and reinforce the effort he put forward as well as to point out alternative opportunities for careers in electronics and areas associated with electronics. What effects will improved information regarding the military have on his future direction and goals?

Information is of key importance in self-determination. Does the student have enough information to make informed decisions regarding his or her values and interests leading to a preferred occupational choice? Certainly, for Jason, a trip to the local community college or technical college would be facilitative to find out more about careers in electronics. Perhaps the additional information will lead him to reexamine his choice of the military and lead to additional exploration at the local university. Perhaps in his visits he will find other occupations to explore. Certainly, career exploration leads to improved self-awareness.

A goal orientation requires the educator to continually assist the student to reexamine and reassess personal strengths and limitations, goals and aspirations. It requires that the educator provide meaningful feedback for decision making in a positive and constructive manner. It requires that the educator assist students in exploring many alternatives and creating a safety net of alternative choices. A goal orientation and a *commitment to future planning* means letting the goals and aspirations of the student drive the individual education program (IEP). Teachers should not rob students of their goals by dismissing them as too hard or impossible. It is much more appropriate and effective for teachers to point out strengths and concerns and provide positive alternatives. The goal must be for students to learn to examine and reexamine themselves, expand their *self-knowledge* and develop the ability to *make decisions* and *self-evaluate* based on improved and refined information. The cumulative effect will be a developing *reality orientation*.

What course of study will Jason decide to pursue during his junior and senior years? Since he is interested in electronics, will he choose to participate in an algebra class? Will he participate in an electronics course in the high school? Will he be in the tech prep program, perhaps in service learning to get some hands-on experience in the community? If he ultimately decides that he wants to attend the community college and major in electronic repair, what support services are available to him to assist him to be successful? To whom must he talk to get those services? How does he go about getting admitted to community college? Are there any community resources that can help him pay for tuition and books to attend community college? Certainly, *understanding community resources* and having the skills of *self-advocacy* (to identify what he needs and get what he wants) will be important to self-determination.

As demonstrated in Jason's scenario, self-determination requires the participation and leadership of students in developing and implementing their goals for the future. As such, self-determination requires that students participate in their own IEP and lead the development of the IEP if at all possible. One of the most effective ways to incorporate self-determination into the educational program of a student is to teach the student the skills of directing his or her own IEP. The IEP is, after all, the cornerstone of special education policy and the tool of accountability. It is also the planning document for the student's education. Martin, Marshall, and Maxson (1993) suggested that self-management of the IEP process holds the opportunity to foster the development of self-determination skills. These authors ask: Where else in the student's school life are choices more important? Secondary-level curricular materials to assist with teaching self-determination, including materials specifically focused on the IEP process, are reviewed in Chapter 5.

What Curricular Strategies Are Available to Specifically Promote Self-Advocacy Skills?

Self-advocacy skills are the skills individuals need to, quite literally, advocate on their own behalf. To advocate means to speak up or defend a cause or a person. By definition, then, instruction to promote self-advocacy will focus on two common threads: how to advocate and what to advocate. Elementary-age students can begin to learn basic self-advocacy skills, but most instructional emphasis in this area will apply during secondary school education. It is not feasible to teach students everything for which they could possibly advocate. However, one particularly important area in which students with disabilities should receive instruction involves the education and transition process itself and student rights and responsibilities within that system. For many students with disabilities, school is a place they are forced to go to do things that someone else decides upon. It is little wonder that motivation becomes a problem.

Students who are approaching transition age can be taught about their rights and responsibilities under the Individuals with Disabilities Education

Act and, more specifically, about the purpose and process involved in transition decision making. As discussed in Chapter 2, the IEP and transition planning meetings provide an ideal vehicle for teaching self-advocacy skills in a meaningful manner. Other topics that could become the cause for which students will need to advocate on their own behalf include the adult services system (disability and general), basic civil and legal rights of citizenship, and specific civil and legal protections available to people with disabilities (e.g., The Americans with Disabilities Act). Such instructional efforts will necessarily deal with both rights and responsibilities.

The curricular strategies for the "how to advocate" side of self-advocacy include instructional emphasis on being assertive but not aggressive; how to communicate effectively in one-on-one, small-group and large-group situations; how to negotiate, compromise, and use persuasion; how to be an effective listener; and how to navigate through systems and bureaucracies. It is evident that each of these is closely tied to the acquisition and emergence of other self-determination skills. For example, a reliable understanding of one's strengths and weaknesses is an important component if one is to actually use strategies such as negotiation and compromise to achieve a desired outcome. Likewise, students need to be able to link such advocacy to specific goals and incorporate it into the problem-solving or decision-making process.

What Is the Role of the Family in Promoting Self-Determination?

Families and caregivers play a critical role in the development of self-determination, and school professionals should work closely with the people in the student's home to achieve this outcome. Turnbull and Turnbull (1996) identified features of families that can serve to facilitate or impede an individual's development of self-determined behaviors, including:

- Family characteristics such as cultural values, beliefs and expectations, and coping styles.

- Family interactions such as role expectations, relationships, cohesion, and adaptability.

- Family functions, including economic, daily care, recreation, socialization, affective, educational/vocational, and self-definition needs.

- Family lifespan issues (including developmental stages of family interactions and functions over time, transitions or changes in family characteristics, composition, cohesion, and function).

There are certain things families and caregivers can do to facilitate young children's attitudes and skills of self-determination beginning in preschool and extending into the elementary school years. According to the National Association for the Education of Young Children, the following parenting and caregiver practices support the development of prosocial skills that ultimately influence abilities of self-determination (Bredekamp, 1987, p. 47):

- Provision of affection and support, comforting children when they cry and reassuring them when they are fearful.

- Support for children's developing independence, helping when needed, but allowing them to do what they are capable of doing and what they want to do for themselves.

- Consideration of each child as a unique person with individual patterns and timing for skill development.

- Provision of activities, interactions, and feedback to develop children's positive self-esteem and positive feelings toward learning.

- Provision of opportunities to develop social skills such as cooperating, helping, negotiating, and talking with persons with whom they are involved in interpersonal problems.

- Facilitating the development of self-control through positive guidance techniques such as modeling expected behaviors, redirecting children to more acceptable activities, and setting clear limits.

- Promoting perseverance, industry, and independence by providing stimulating, motivating activities; encouraging individual choices; allowing as much time as is needed for children to complete their work; and ensuring private time with close friends and loved ones.

- Setting clear limits in a positive manner and involving children in establishing rules and in problem solving.

Davis and Wehmeyer (1991) provided the following specific "10 steps to self-determination" for parents of children with disabilities:

1. Walk the tightrope between protection and independence. Allow your son or daughter to explore his or her world. This may mean biting your lip and watching from the kitchen window when your child first meets the neighbor's kids, instead of running out to supervise. While there are obvious limits to this, all parents have to "let go," and it is never easy.

2. Children need to learn that what they say or do is important and can have influence on others. This involves allowing risk-taking and exploration. Encourage your child to ask questions and express opinions. Involvement in family discussions and decision-making sessions is one way of providing this opportunity to learn.

3. Self-worth and self-confidence are critical factors in the development of self-determination. Model your own sense of positive self-esteem to your child. Tell your child that she is important by spending time with her. Again, involve her in family activities and in family decisions.

4. Don't run away from questions from your child about differences related to his disability. That doesn't mean, however, to focus on the negative side of the condition. Stress that everyone is individual, encourage your child's unique abilities, and help him to accept unavoidable limitations.

5. Recognize the process of reaching goals, don't just emphasize outcomes. Children need to learn to work toward goals. For older children, encourage skills like organization and goal-setting by modeling these behaviors. Make lists or hang a marker board in the laundry room which shows the daily schedule for each family member. Talk about the steps you are going to use to complete a task and involve them in tasks leading to family goals, such as planning for a vacation.

6. Schedule opportunities for interactions with children of different ages and backgrounds. This could be in day care centers, schools, churches, and when playing in the neighborhood. Start early in finding chances for your son or daughter to participate in activities that help all children realize everyone is unique.

7. Set realistic but ambitious expectations. The adage that our goals should extend just beyond our reach is true here. Take an active role in your child's educational experience. Be familiar with his or her reading ability and identify books that provide enough challenge to move to the next reading level. Be sure you don't just force activities which lead to frustration, but don't assume that all of the progress should occur at school.

8. Allow your child to take responsibility for her own actions. . . successes and failures. Provide valid reasons for doing things, instead of simply saying "because I said so!" Providing explanations provides the opportunity for the child to make an activity his own.

9. Don't leave choice-making opportunities to chance. Take every opportunity to allow your child to make choices; what she wears, what is served for dinner, or where the family goes for vacation. And, although this is not always practical or possible, make sure that these choice opportunities are meaningful. For example, for most children choosing between broccoli or cauliflower is not a choice! Also, when offering choices, make sure that the child's decision is honored.

10. Provide honest, positive feedback. Focus on the behavior or task that needs to be changed. Don't make your child feel like a failure. For example, if your son or daughter attempts to complete a school activity, say a math sheet, but is unable to do so, phrase the feedback so that he or she knows that the failure was specific to the worksheet and not in him or her. We all learn from our mistakes, but only if they are structured so that they do not lead us to believe that the problem is within us. (pp. 1–2)

If the outcome that all children with disabilities leave school as self-determined young adults is to be achieved, educators must begin by providing instructional activities and environments that promote the development of component elements of self-determination while children are in early childhood and elementary school programs. This will require attention not only to school activities and structure, but also to the establishment of partnerships with students' families.

What Is the Role of School Administrators in Promoting Self-Determination?

School administrators are responsible for implementing and managing educational reform in our schools. Self-determination will not become an integral part of the school environment if it is not supported and encouraged by school administrators. School administrators assist in establishing the tone and help to establish the environment of the building. Establishing a school environment that promotes self-determination is an extremely important issue. Too often systems are set up to foster dependency and hinder personal control (Sands & Wehmeyer, 1996). Control is a major issue in today's schools, and self-determination means allowing students and faculty appropriate control over their own learning and working environments as well as establishing a more interactive and cooperative environment. Sharing decision making with students and faculty as well as providing a safe environment that nurtures individual uniqueness of all kinds is no small accomplishment. The changes discussed here represent systemic change in the interaction of administrators, teachers and students inside the educational system.

Following are some ideas to assist schools and school administrators in planning to implement educational reform focused on student self-determination. These ideas focus on leadership, goal setting, empowerment, and resources.

Administrator Interactions with Students

• School administrators can work to systematically provide students with opportunities to exercise choice throughout planning, implementing, and evaluation of the school. Abery and Stancliffe (1996) suggested that students should have a voice in decision-making matters such as curriculum content, course selection, scheduling, governance, and extracurricular activities. This process will teach students responsibility as well as decision making. Included in this process of site-based decision making is student involvement in hiring of faculty and staff.

• School administrators may choose to support student inservice instruction on goal setting and the development of individualized education programs (IEPs for students with special education needs).

• School administrators can support utilizing the entire community as a learning laboratory. Research has demonstrated that student decisions are often based on experience, and many students, including students with disabilities, lack life experience. Support for programming such as community-based work experience and service learning allows students to gather and process information for decision making and problem solving.

• School administrators can explore curriculum options available to students with disabilities. All students should have options for curricular choices that make school meaningful. Currently, school-to-work initiatives and tech prep curricula offer students meaningful vocational alternatives to the college prep curriculum. However, too often students with disabilities are eliminated from both the vocational education and college prep courses of study in favor of a general curriculum that does not prepare them to participate in life after high school. School administrators can assist students to become self-determined by making sure that every student has access to a meaningful educational program and that this program has taken the student's needs, wants, goals, and aspirations into account.

- School administrators can work to establish a common belief in the importance of self-determination for all students and staff. Even though change in our schools tends to be incremental, a commitment to the importance of self-determination can be an integral part of the school's strategic plan.

Administrator Interactions with Faculty

- School administrators may support inservice training for teachers in strategies to share choice making, problem solving, and decision making with students. In addition, school administrators may choose to support inservice training for teachers in strategies related to implementation of a self-determination curriculum. Hoffman and Field (1994) identified the following 10 cornerstones as the foundation for a self-determination curriculum. These may also provide a good starting place to infuse instructional strategies that are consistent with self-determination into the school curriculum.

    1. Establish a co-learner role for teachers.
    2. Emphasize modeling as an instructional strategy.
    3. Use cooperative learning techniques.
    4. Use experiential learning strategies.
    5. Promote integrated or inclusive environments.
    6. Obtain support from family and friends.
    7. Foster an open, accepting classroom environment.
    8. Incorporate interdisciplinary teaching.
    9. Use humor appropriately.
    10. Capitalize on teachable moments.

- Many school administrators may need to reexamine practices related to supervision of faculty in implementing a model of self-determination in the school. A model of self-determination suggests a more interactive and collaborative form of staff supervision and evaluation. In this collaborative model, performance is based on mutually identified goals. The role of the administrator may include identifying resources, asking questions, providing information, listening, and providing feedback to teachers (Field & Hoffman, 1996). If teachers are to model self-determined behavior for students, the skills and attitudes of self-determination must be supported for them by administrators.

- School administrators can lead a reexamination of what it means to graduate from high school. Is graduation more than the number of credits the student earns? How can we provide students credit for a diversity of opportunities within a tight fiscal budget?

- School administrators may choose to provide minigrants for faculty to explore the integration of shared decision-making practices in their classrooms with students.

- Finally, school administrators can work to provide mentoring and role modeling to staff and students in self-determination. Field and Hoffman (1996) suggested that role modeling by those in leadership positions (e.g., principals and superintendents) is particularly important to encourage self-determination within a school. Self-determination will be strengthened or weakened on a school-wide basis depending on the types of administrative models (e. g., self-determined, authoritarian, passive) to which students and teachers are exposed. One strategy that has been successful in mentoring teachers to promote self-determination for staff and students is the coteaching model. This model pairs less experienced teachers with mentors who are more experienced role models in promoting self-determination (Field & Hoffman, 1996).

To address self-determination in the school, school administrators must be goal oriented, student focused, reinforcing of efforts to change the status quo, and willing to attempt creative answers to difficult problems. Administrators must be willing to applaud the attempt and reinforce the effort of expanding student and faculty self-determination.

What Noncurricular Strategies Are Available to Promote Self-Determination?

Noncurricular strategies involve *how* we teach self-determination. Such strategies relate to the teaching techniques we employ in the classroom, how the classroom is organized and set up, what rules exist, and what extracurricular opportunities are available. An effective overall strategy to promote self-determination will incorporate the utilization of nontraditional, student-directed models of teaching and learning presented in environments that promote choice and student involvement, including community-based learning experiences. These efforts will also include the use of peer and adult mentors.

Agran (1997) stated that "rather than continue to rely on an instructional model in which the teacher is given full responsibility for determining when, what, why, where, and how a student will learn, we are beginning to realize that there may be marked advantages in having the student more actively involved in educational decision-making, as well as the delivery of instruction itself." Many of the components of self-determination, from self-awareness and self-regulation to autonomy, simply cannot be taught using traditional teacher-directed models. It is imperative that teachers use different models of instruction, such as student self-management procedures, role playing, brainstorming, and group investigation.

A predominant model employed by many teachers in special education involves the use of contingency management or applied behavior analysis procedures. While these procedures have enabled students with even the most significant disabilities to learn and gain independence, they have, paradoxically, been partially responsible for the limited opportunities for control and choice for students. Instructional emphasis has too often been placed on compliance and teacher control and too infrequently on self-control and self-management. It is not that the particular strategies are, in and of themselves, incompatible with the development of self-determination, but instead that they have been used in such a way as to limit this outcome. Gothelf and Brown (1996) discussed the effects of these instructional strategies on self-determination and pointed out that task analyses rarely include choices in a process and basically ignore steps in the process where self-determination skills could be taught. They suggest, as an example, that a task analysis of making a sandwich might be expanded to include choosing between wheat or white bread, indicating preferences in mustard or mayonnaise, and allowing for the termination of the activity if the student is not hungry or wants something different. Likewise, the excessive use of prompting can lead to a dependence on others if not implemented carefully. Prompts can be linked with natural cues, however, and faded to provide the student the opportunity to control his or her action.

This illustrates the importance of employing self-management strategies, such as self-instruction, self-monitoring, and self-reinforcement. There are a large number of studies showing that self-management procedures have the benefit of teaching targeted skills and providing increased motivation and control for the student. Unfortunately, such strategies remain essentially marginalized; they are rarely used except when all else has failed or in response to extreme behavior problems.

Another important component is the use of mentoring as a means to teach self-determination. Students can be matched or paired with successful adults who have a similar disability to form a mentoring relationship. These adult mentors provide a model of success in the community and can be a good way to teach and reinforce the importance of such things as goal-setting, decision-making and problem-solving skills, and other self-determination skills.

An often-used component of many self-determination programs is work and other community experiences. Such experiences provide students with disabilities with opportunities to explore options in postsecondary education, employment, housing, transportation, recreation and leisure, and policy making by using frequent community-based learning experiences. This enables students to develop preferences and make informed choices and decisions based on their own experiences.

In addition to instructional methods, the environment in which children and youth learn is important. In addition to providing community-based instruction, teachers can ensure that the classroom environment is conducive to promoting self-determination. Brotherson, Cook, Cunconan-Lahr, and Wehmeyer (1995) pointed out that "the built environment influences activity by facilitating certain actions and limiting others. Signage, circulation pathways, storage placement and height, furnishings and equipment selection, arrangement and wall hangings, and decorations have both direct impact and symbolic connotations" (p. 5). For example, the absence of a clear pathway to a defined play area may result in underutilization, even if that path is not actually blocked. Likewise, placing art work and signage appropriate to the child's capabilities (e.g., word, pictures, pictographs) sends a message that this is the child's environment and provides the opportunity for choice and decision making. Classrooms that have materials stored where students can access them freely and without assistance, where children have a voice in seating arrangements and the physical layout of the instructional areas, and which provide multiple opportunities for choices will be conducive to promoting self-determination.

CONCLUSION

Promoting self-determination for students requires us to closely examine our curriculum offerings to ensure that self-determination skills are taught and that students have ample opportunities to exercise those skills. Encouraging self-determination in students affects both curriculum content and the instructional strategies that are used to help students acquire knowledge and skills. Self-determination curriculum content and practices need to be addressed in both classroom and school-wide settings and at all educational levels, from early childhood through adult education. A team effort is needed to help students become more self-determined. Students, parents, teachers, administrators, and other school staff all play important roles in helping to reshape educational efforts to support student self-determination.

REFERENCES

Abery, B., & Stancliffe, R. (1996). The ecology of self-determination. In D. J. Sands & M. L. Wehmeyer (Eds.), *Self-determination across the life span: Independence and choice for people with disabilities*, (pp.109–143). Baltimore: Paul H. Brookes.

Abery, B., & Zajac, R. (1996). Self-determination as a goal of early childhood and elementary education. In D. J. Sands & M. L. Wehmeyer (Eds.), *Self-determination across the life span: Independence and choice for people with disabilities*, (pp. 165–192). Baltimore: Paul H. Brookes.

Agran, M. (1997). *Student-directed learning: A handbook on self-management.* Pacific Grove, CA: Brooks/Cole.

Biller, E. F. (1985). *Understanding and guiding the career development of adolescents and young adults with learning disabilities.* Springfield, IL: Charles C Thomas.

Bredekamp, S. (1987). *Developmentally appropriate practice in early childhood programs servicing children from birth through age 8.* Washington, DC: National Association for the Education of Young Children.

Brotherson, M. J., Cook, C., Cunconan-Lahr, R., & Wehmeyer, M. L. (1995). Policy supporting self-determination in the environments of children with disabilities. *Education and Training in Mental Retardation and Developmental Disabilities, 30,* 3–14. (ERIC Document Reproduction Service No. EJ 501 296)

Brown, F., Appel, C., Corsi, L., & Wenig, B., (1993). Choice diversity for people with severe disabilities. *Education and Training in Mental Retardation, 28,* 318–326. (ERIC Document Reproduction Service No. EJ 477 649)

Davis, S., & Wehmeyer, M. L. (1991). *Ten steps to independence: Promoting self-determination in the home.* Arlington, TX: The Arc.

Doll, B., Sands, D. J., Wehmeyer, M. L., & Palmer, S. (1996). Promoting the development and acquisition of self-determined behavior. In D. J. Sands & M. L. Wehmeyer (Eds.), *Self-determination across the life span: Independence and choice for people with disabilities,* (pp. 63–88). Baltimore: Paul H. Brookes.

Fairweather, J. S., & Shaver, D. M. (1991). Making the transition to post-secondary education and training. *Exceptional Children, 5,* 264–270. (ERIC Document Reproduction Service No. EJ 421 436)

Field, S. (1996). Self-determination instructional strategies for youth with learning disabilities. *Journal of Learning Disabilities, 29*(1), 40–52. (ERIC Document Reproduction Service No. EJ 517 928)

Field, S., & Hoffman, A. (1996). Increasing the ability of educators to support youth self-determination. In L. E. Powers, G. H. S. Singer, & J. Sowers (Eds.) *Making our way: Building self-confidence among youth with disabilities* (pp. 171–187). Baltimore: Paul H. Brookes.

Gothelf, C. R., & Brown, F. (1996). Instructional support for self-determination in individuals with profound disabilities who are deaf-blind. In D. H. Lehr & F. Brown (Eds.), *People with disabilities who challenge the system,* (pp. 355–377). Baltimore: Paul H. Brookes.

Hasazi, S. Gordon, L., & Roe, C. (1985). Factors associated with the employment status of handicapped youth exiting high school from 1979–1983. *Exceptional Children, 51,* 455–469. (ERIC Document Reproduction Service No. EJ 316 948)

Hoffman, A., & Field, S. (1994). Promoting self-determination through effective curriculum development. *Intervention in School and Clinic, 30*(3), 134–141. (ERIC Document Reproduction Service No. EJ 497 546)

Martin, J. E., Marshall, L. H., & Maxon, L. L. (1993). Transition policy: Infusing self-determination and self-advocacy into transition programs. *Career Development for Exceptional Individuals, 16*(1), 53–58. (ERIC Document Reproduction Service No. EJ 465 409)

Reid, D. H., Parsons, M. B., & Green, C. W. (1991). *Providing choices and preferences for persons who have severe handicaps: Practical procedures for good times.* Morganton, NC: Habilitative Management Consultants.

Rojewski, J. W. (1996). Educational and occupational aspirations of high school seniors with learning disabilities. *Exceptional Children, 62,* 463–476. (ERIC Document Reproduction Service No. EJ 519 867)

Sands, D. J., Adams, L., & Stout, D. M. (1995). A statewide exploration of the nature and use of curriculum in special education. *Exceptional Children, 62,* 68–83. (ERIC Document Reproduction Service No. EJ 511 822)

Sands, D. J., & Wehmeyer, M. L. (1996). Future directions in self-determination: Redefining policies, systems and responses. In D. J. Sands & M. L. Wehmeyer (Eds.), *Self-determination across the life span: Independence and choice for people with disabilities,* (pp. 325–338). Baltimore: Paul H. Brookes.

Shure, M. B. (1992). *I Can Problem Solve: An interpersonal cognitive problem-solving program.* Champaign, IL: Research Press.

Siegel, S., Robert, M., Waxman, M., & Gaylord-Ross, R. (1992). A follow-along study of participants in a longitudinal transition program for youths with mild disabilities. *Exceptional Children, 58,* 346–356. (ERIC Document Reproduction Service No. EJ 442 994)

Sitlington, P., Frank, A., & Carson, R. (1992). Are adolescents with learning disabilities successfully crossing the bridge into adult life? *Learning Disabilities Quarterly, 13,* 97–111. (ERIC Document Reproduction Service No. EJ 411 771)

Smith, D. D. (1989). *Teaching students with learning and behavior problems* (2nd ed.). Upper Saddle River, NJ: Prentice Hall.

Super, D. E. (1983). Assessment in career guidance: Toward truly developmental counseling. *The Personnel and Guidance Journal, 61,* 555–561. (ERIC Document Reproduction Service No. EJ 285 133)

Turnbull, A. P., & Turnbull, H. R. (1996). Self-determination within a culturally responsive family systems perspective: Balancing the family mobile. In L. E. Powers, G. H. S. Singer, & J. Sowers (Eds.), *Promoting self-competence in children and youth with disabilities: On the road to autonomy* (pp. 195–220). Baltimore: Paul H. Brookes.

Wagner, M. Newman, L, D'Amico, R., Jay, E., Butler-Nalin, P., Marder, C., & Cox, R. (1991). *Youth with disabilities: How are they doing? The first comprehensive report from the National Longitudinal Transition Study of Special Education Students.* Menlo Park, CA: SRI International.

Wehmeyer, M. L. (1993). Perceptual and psychological factors in career decision-making of adolescents with and without cognitive disabilities. *Career Development for Exceptional Individuals, 16*(2), 135–146. (ERIC Document Reproduction Service No. EJ 477 686)

Wehmeyer, M. L., & Kelchner, K. (1994 December). Interpersonal cognitive problem-solving skills of individuals with mental retardation. *Education and Training in Mental Retardation and Developmental Disabilities,* 265–278. (ERIC Document Reproduction Service No. EJ 493 104)

Wehmeyer, M., & Schwartz, M. A. (1997). Self-determination and positive adult outcomes: A follow-up study of youth with mental retardation and learning disabilities. *Exceptional Children, 63,* 245–255.

Self-Determination Instructional Materials Review

The purpose of this chapter is to

- Provide a review of curriculum materials available to support self-determination instruction.

During recent years, several educators from across the country have developed self-determination materials. A few of these are just now starting to appear in the catalogs of commercial publishers. The rest are available from the authors or their organizations. Educators face a difficult task finding information about most of these resources. Access to these materials remains limited due to the difficulty in finding them.

An increasing number of educators are looking for ways to teach their students self-determination skills. No one curriculum or lesson package can meet all of an educator's needs. Educators want and need various curricular ideas and methodology. Thus, the purpose of this chapter is to provide a concise review of self-determination instructional materials so educators can quickly locate resources that will assist them in implementing self-determination-oriented instructional practices.

This chapter was developed by J. E. Martin, T. L. Miller, L. Huber Marshall, G. J. Kregar, and W. Hughes with support from several Colorado Springs educators who assisted in reviewing curriculum packages, including Jamie Finn, Patty Jerman, and Cindy Tarrant. The chapter was developed with partial support from Grant No. H158Q40027 from the U.S. Department of Education, Office of Special Education and Rehabilitative Services (OSERS). Opinions expressed herein do not necessarily reflect those of OSERS. The authors would like to thank Ben Lignugaris/Kraft for his assistance in developing the curriculum review process.

How Was This Review Completed?

A team of university and public school secondary special educators jointly conducted and wrote this review using a five-step process. First, all federally funded self-determination model demonstration projects were asked to submit a copy of the self-determination instructional materials developed. In addition, efforts were made to obtain information about self-determination products developed through other sources.

Second, a detailed curriculum description form was developed and the authors worked with this form until agreement was reached on review of a lesson package. Third, two team members independently reviewed each lesson package. The two-person team then met and discussed each item on the description form until they reached consensus. Fourth, a description of the review was sent to the primary author of each curriculum to ask for corrections and additions to the initial review. Fifth, the information the authors provided was inserted into the review as long as it related to our preestablished categories.

What Is In This Review?

A descriptive review of self-determination instructional lesson packages is provided. Sufficient information is provided so you can decide whether you want to further examine or obtain a particular curriculum lesson package. Because what is useful to one educator may not apply to the needs of another, and what one educator likes another may not, a qualitative judgment was not made in this review.

The descriptive review contains five sections. Each section contains numerous possible subsections and detailed descriptors. The review of each curriculum lesson package contains only those items determined by the review team that apply to that specific package. The following sections and subsections were included in each review:

Abstract

1. Program Description
   a. Type of material
   b. Students
   c. Ages
   d. Other
   e. Self-determination content

2. Materials Description
   a. Materials provided
   b. Materials packaging and presentation
   c. Equipment needed
   d. Cost

3. Instructional Delivery
   a. Setting
   b. Instructional grouping
   c. Delivery method
   d. Leader
   e. Number of leaders
   f. Leader role
   g. Leader training
   h. Lesson sequence
   i. Frequency of lesson use
   j. Required preparation
   k. Number of lessons
   l. Lesson time

4. Instructional Components
   a. Objectives
   b. Prerequisite skills
   c. Quality of instruction
   d. Performance evaluation frequency
   e. Performance evaluation type
   f. Learner activities
   g. Generalization

5. Research and Field Testing
   a. Research
   b. Field testing

Do You Know of Any Additional Materials?

If you discover additional self-determination curriculum lesson packages that are not included in this review, please let us know. We will try to secure a copy and include a review in future revisions of this chapter. Send information about additional self-determination curriculum materials to: Jim Martin, Self-Determination Projects, Special Education Program, University of Colorado at Colorado Springs, P.O. Box 7150, Colorado Springs, CO 80933-7150. Telephone: 719/262-3627 or e-mail: jmartin@mail.uccs.edu.

MATERIALS REVIEWED

A MAZE TO AMAZE: TRANSITION PLANNING FOR YOUTH WITH DISABILITIES
A Video and Manual for Constructing a Transition IEP Meeting

Susan J. McAlonan and Patricia A. Longo

Susan J. McAlonan and Patricia A. Longo
Colorado Department of Education, Special Education Services Unit
201 East Colfax Avenue
Denver, CO 80203

Abstract

The *A Maze to Amaze* video demonstrates an IEP meeting that focuses on transition planning. It represents a shift in IEP planning from a disability base to a future planning base, with the student's desired future situations as the focus. The meeting becomes student centered as the student and family become active participants. The manual is designed to give special educators practice in translating the philosophy of focusing on students' self-determination and planning for the future into the requirements of the law and the forms the law requires within the IEP process. The manual will assist educators and service providers to understand the IEP/transition planning process, assess the current IEP process, review examples of transition plans and IEP forms, review examples of appropriate transition goals and objectives, practice writing transition goals and objectives, and develop self-determination practices for students.

1. Program Description

Type of Material

- Teacher instruction or training

Students

- Noncategorical

Ages

- Middle/junior high school
- Senior high school

Other

- Educators
- Facilitators

Self-Determination Content

- Personal self-advocacy: Acting on one's knowledge of oneself and one's rights
- Goal setting: Deciding desired outcomes
- Person-centered planning: Actively participating in planning activities such as planning one's own IEP
- Employment: Jobs, careers
- Education: Classes, sports, clubs, postsecondary education
- Housing and daily living: Home setting, daily living skills
- Personal: Recreation, leisure, legal, medical, health and wellness, relationships
- Community: Transportation, adult services, volunteering

2. Materials Description

Materials Provided

- Replicable worksheets or masters
- Instructional video

Materials Packaging and Presentation

- Three-ring binder

Equipment Needed

- VCR and monitor

Cost

- $50

3. Instructional Delivery

Setting

- Not specified

Instructional Grouping

- Not specified

Delivery Method

- Not specified

Leader

- Not specified

Number of Leaders

- Not specified

Leader Role

- Not specified

Leader Training

- Not specified

Lesson Sequence

- Not specified

Frequency of Lesson Use

- Not specified

Required Preparation

- Not specified

Number of Lessons

- Not specified

Lesson Time

- Not specified

4. Instructional Components

Objectives

- Not specified

Prerequisite Skills

- Not specified

Quality of Instruction

- Not specified

Performance Evaluation Frequency

- Not specified

Performance Evaluation Type

- Not specified

Learner Activities

- Not specified

Generalization

- Not specified

5. Research and Field Testing

Research

- Not specified

Field Testing

- Not specified

BECOME YOUR OWN EXPERT: SELF-ADVOCACY CURRICULUM FOR INDIVIDUALS WITH LEARNING DISABILITIES

Winnelle D. Carpenter

Winnelle D. Carpenter
Minnesota Educational Services at Capitol View Center
70 West County Road, B2
Little Canada, MN 55117-1402
1-800-848-4912 ext. 2401

Abstract

Become Your Own Expert is used to teach high school students with learning disabilities self-advocacy skills during a 1-semester course. The self-advocacy skills that are directly taught in this curriculum include identifying individual academic strengths and weaknesses and learning styles and setting goals for completing high school and continuing postsecondary education and training. In addition, students learn about classroom and workplace accommodations that help them be successful and about federal and transition laws that support them in their efforts. The skill development activities employ a variety of instructional techniques and strategies such as structured group problem solving, videotaped self-evaluations, site visits to postsecondary programs, and activities involving postsecondary students and adults with learning disabilities. A corresponding parent program accompanies this curriculum, and many parents may learn how to support students while they acquire new skills.

1. Program Description

Type of Material

- Instructional tool
- Assessment tool (ordered extra)

Students

- With learning disabilities

Ages

- Middle/junior high school (9th grade and up)
- Senior high school

Other

- Families

Self-Determination Content

- Self-awareness: Identifying information about self—interests, strengths, weaknesses
- Personal self-advocacy: Acting on one's knowledge of oneself and one's rights
- Housing and daily living: Home setting, daily living skills
- Goal-setting: Deciding on desired outcomes
- Self-evaluation: Comparing one's performance to a standard
- Adjustment: Making adaptations to achieve desired outcomes
- Person-centered planning: Actively participating in planning activities such as planning one's own IEP
- Making choices and decisions
- Employment: Jobs, careers
- Education: Classes, sports, clubs, postsecondary education
- Community: Transportation, adult services, volunteering

2. Materials Description

Materials Provided

- Replicable worksheets or masters
- Guide with background and overview
- Guide with directions for facilitating

Materials Packaging and Presentation

- Three-ring binder

Equipment Needed

- Overhead projector
- Flip chart
- VCR and monitor
- Camcorder

Cost

- Less than $100

3. Instructional Delivery

Setting

- Special education classes

Instructional Grouping

- Not specified

Delivery Method

- Leader presents information
- Discovery/experiential: Participants complete activities related to objectives
- Group process: Participants interact with group members in activities related to objectives
- Community-based instruction: Experiences in the community

Leader

- Special educator
- School psychologist
- Social worker or counselor

Number of Leaders
- Two: Team approach

Leader Role
- Instructor: Leader directed
- Facilitator: Facilitates group interaction

Leader Training
- Not specified (author states teacher should have LD certification)

Lesson Sequence
- Set sequence

Frequency of Lesson Use
- Daily in a 1-semester course

Required Preparation
- Secure community sites
- Schedule guest speakers
- Order other curricular and assessment materials
- Make copies and visual aids
- Gather community information

Number of Lessons
- 43

Lesson Time
- 50 minutes (five times/week for a semester)

4. Instructional Components

Objectives
- Objectives stated
- Objectives measurable: Observable behavior, conditions, criteria

Prerequisite Skills
- None identified

Quality of Instruction
- Targeted skills are clearly identified
- Skill sequence
- All activities align with objectives
- Examples and nonexamples used to teach concepts
- Cumulative review
- Spaced repetition
- Practice opportunities provided for targeted skills
- Feedback procedures provided

- Remedial procedures provided
- Modifications suggested for populations

Performance Evaluation Frequency
- Pretest and/or posttest

Performance Evaluation Type
- Criterion-referenced assessment (measurement of skills compared to performance criterion)
- Rating scales checklists—others indicate occurrence or magnitude of behavior
- Direct observation and recording: Observer uses measuring system to assess behavior as it occurs

Learner Activities
- Listening to information presented verbally (lecture)
- Reading and writing
- Group discussion
- Role play
- Games
- Community activities
- Question/answer
- Videos
- Mentoring
- Homework
- Learning or self-management strategies
- Cooperative learning
- Peer coaching

Generalization
- Rehearsal of behavior to approximate real situations
- Practice in more than one setting
- Practice rules for when to apply skills
- Conditional discriminations taught
- Frequent review of skills or incorporated into new skills
- Discussions of situations relevant to students in which they might use behavior

5. Research and Field Testing

Research
- User feedback: Users provide feedback on value of program

Field Testing
- Field test reported, but no outcome data presented

BECOMING THE ME I WANT TO BE, BUILDING SKILLS, AND MAKING CHOICES

Various Authors

Spina Bifida Association of Kentucky
Kosair Charities Centre
982 Eastern Parkway
Louisville, KY 40217
502-637-7363

Abstract

The Transition to Independence Project (Project TIP) developed these three manuals to encourage youth with disabilities to develop the skills needed to become self-determined adults. The three booklets are designed to raise awareness about the importance and fundamental aspects of self-determination. *Being the Me I Want to Be* is designed for children and young teens with adult involvement and support. *Making Choices* is for older teens and young adults working with a mentor. *Building Skills* accompanies the first two and is for the adult who is helping teach the concepts. Together, these booklets define spina bifida, provide care guidelines, and show how the three ideas of development, autonomy, and choice can be incorporated into an awareness-building program.

1. Program Description

Type of Material

- Instructional tool

Students

- Children and youth with spina bifida

Ages

- Middle/junior high school
- Senior high school
- 18–21 years old

Other

- Parents
- Families
- Other professionals

Self-Determination Content

- Self-awareness: Identifying information about self—interests, strengths, weaknesses
- Personal self-advocacy: Acting on one's knowledge of oneself and one's rights
- Self-efficacy: Belief that one can accomplish one's goals
- Goal setting: Deciding on desired outcomes
- Self-evaluation: Comparing one's performance to a standard
- Making choices and decisions
- Employment: Jobs, careers
- Education: Classes, sports, clubs, postsecondary education
- Housing and daily living: Home setting, daily living skills
- Personal: Recreation, leisure, legal, medical, health and wellness, relationships
- Community: Transportation, adult services, volunteering

2. Materials Description

Materials Provided

- Consumable written materials
- Guide with background and overview
- Guide with directions for facilitating

Materials Packaging and Presentation

- Spiral bound

Equipment Needed

- Not specified

Cost

- No information provided

3. Instructional Delivery

Setting

- Not specified

Instructional Grouping

- Not specified

Delivery Method

- Discovery/experiential: Participants complete activities related to objectives

Leader

- Parent
- Individual with disability

Number of Leaders

- Not specified

Leader Role

- Not specified

Leader Training

- Not specified

Lesson Sequence

- Not specified

Frequency of Lesson Use

- Not specified

Required Preparation

- Not specified

Number of Lessons

- Not specified

Lesson Time

- Not specified

4. Instructional Components

Objectives

- Not specified

Prerequisite Skills

- None identified

Quality of Instruction

- Targeted skills are clearly identified

Performance Evaluation Frequency

- Pretest and/or posttest

Performance Evaluation Type

- Self-report: Student indicates occurrence or magnitude of behavior

Learner Activities

- Listening to information presented verbally (lecture)
- Reading and writing
- Mentoring

Generalization

- None reported

5. Research and Field Testing

Research

- Expert appraisal: Material given appraisal by area experts

Field Testing

- Not reported

BECOMING SELF-DETERMINED

Thomas Holub

Thomas Holub
Madison Metropolitan School District
West Attendance Area
30 Ash Street
Madison, WI 53705
608-261-9500

Abstract

This curriculum involves students in activities to enable them to learn how to make choices. It teaches students to reflect upon themselves and apply their experiences to establish work and adult life goals. The curriculum consists of seven sections that cover such topics as personal maintenance and self-knowledge, home management and safety, time management, budgeting, occupational skills, life planning, and student-directed/self-instruction. Under each domain, various lesson plans are presented that the teacher can use to help prepare a lesson.

1. Program Description

Type of Material
- Instructional tool

Students
- With mild or moderate learning disabilities or developmental disabilities

Ages
- Not specified

Other
- Not specified

Self-Determination Content
- Self-awareness: Identifying information about self—interests, strengths, weaknesses
- Goal-setting: Deciding on desired outcomes, use of a transitional baseline methodology
- Making choices and decisions
- Employment: Jobs, careers
- Housing and daily living: Home setting, daily living skills
- Employment: Jobs, careers
- Community: Transportation, adult services, volunteering

2. Materials Description

Materials Provided
- Guide with directions for facilitating activities

Materials Packaging and Presentation
- Bound in three-ring binder

Equipment Needed
- Not specified

Cost
- $89.95

3. Instructional Delivery

Setting
- Not specified

Instructional Grouping
- Not specified

Delivery Method
- Leader presents information
- Discovery/experiential: Participants complete activities related to objectives
- Group process: Participants interact with group members in activities related to objectives

Leader
- Facilitator or student

Number of Leaders
- No requirement

Leader Role
- Not specified

Leader Training
- Not specified

Lesson Sequence
- Not specified

Frequency of Lesson Use
- Not specified

> Lessons, leadership and sequence have varying dimensional characteristics. Specific details are established (i.e., timing, leadership) when the groups are assembled.

Required Preparation
- None

Number of Lessons
- 91

Lesson Time
- Not specified

4. Instructional Components

Objectives
- Objectives stated

Prerequisite Skills
- Interest in self-determination-related skills and knowledge

Quality of Instruction
- Targeted skills are clearly identified
- All activities align with objectives
- Practice opportunities provided for targeted skills

Performance Evaluation Frequency
- Not specified

Performance Evaluation Type
- Daily slef-evaluation

Learner Activities
- Listening to information presented verbally (lecture)
- Group discussion
- Role play
- Community activities
- Question/answer

Generalization
- Not specified

5. Research and Field Testing

Research
- None reported

Field Testing
- Field test reported, but no outcome data presented. Longitudinal data not yet available. Qualitative, short-term outcomes and comments are available upon request.

CHOICEMAKER SELF-DETERMINATION CURRICULUM: CHOOSING EMPLOYMENT GOALS

Laura Huber Marshall, James E. Martin, Laurie Lee Maxson, and Patty Jerman

Sopris West, Inc.
4093 Specialty Place
Longmont, CO 80504
1-800-547-6747

Abstract

Choosing Employment Goals helps students identify their employment interests, skills, and limits and establish an employment goal. *Choosing Employment Goals* is made up of three lesson categories, which are designed to be infused into existing employment programs and academic courses in whatever order the teacher desires. The first lesson set teaches a general process for choosing goals, which teachers may introduce for any transition area. To help with this, students watch the video "Choosing Goals" as an introduction to the choosing goals process. The second component of the package is designed to be infused into experiential vocational programs. Here students identify their employment interests, skills, and limits and match them to environmental and supervisor demands. The third section is designed to be infused into academic course content. Here students examine various job clusters, conduct "dream job" research, conduct informational interviews, and, if needed, complete a shadowing experience. Step-by-step forms are available to assist students through this process. *Choosing Employment Goals* is intended for all students, including those with mild to moderate learning disabilities, cognitive disabilities, and behavior problems. Included is the ChoiceMaker Self-Determination Assessment for pre-post student progress measurement.

1. Program Description

Type of Material
- Assessment tool
- Instructional tool

Students
- Without disabilities
- Noncategorical

Ages
- Senior high school
- 18–21 years old

Other
- Not specified

Self-Determination Content
- Self-awareness: Identifying information about self—interests, strengths, weaknesses
- Personal self-advocacy: Acting on one's knowledge of oneself and one's rights
- Goal setting: Deciding on desired outcomes
- Self-evaluation: Comparing one's performance to a standard
- Self-efficacy: Belief that one can accomplish one's goals
- Making choices and decisions
- Employment: Jobs, careers
- Education: Classes, sports, clubs, postsecondary education
- Housing and daily living: Home setting, daily living skills
- Personal: Recreation, leisure, legal, medical, health and wellness, relationships
- Community: Transportation, adult services, volunteering

2. Materials Description

Materials Provided
- Replicable worksheets or masters
- Instructional video
- Guide with background and overview
- Guide with directions for facilitating

Materials Packaging and Presentation
- Three-ring binder

Equipment Needed
- VCR and monitor
- Overhead projector

Cost
- $95

3. Instructional Delivery

Setting
- General or special education class
- Community

Instructional Grouping
- Not specified

Delivery Method
- Leader presents information
- Discovery/experiential: Participants complete activities related to objectives
- Group process: Participants interact with group members in activities related to objectives
- Community-based instruction: Experiences in the community

Leader
- Not specified

Number of Leaders
- Not specified

Leader Role
- Instructor: Leader-directed
- Facilitator: Facilitates group interaction

Leader Training
- Not specified

Lesson Sequence
- Flexible sequence

Frequency of Lesson Use
- Flexible

Required Preparation
- Make copies
- Secure community sites

Number of Lessons
- Varies: Designed for the teacher to pick and choose what matches existing program

Lesson Time
- Varies

4. Instructional Components

Objectives
- Objectives stated

Prerequisite Skills
- None identified

Quality of Instruction
- Targeted skills are clearly identified
- Skill sequence
- All activities align with objectives
- Cumulative review
- Spaced repetition
- Practice opportunities provided for targeted skills
- Feedback procedures provided
- Examples used to teach concepts

Performance Evaluation Frequency
- Pretest and/or posttest

- Daily, weekly, or other regular assessment

Performance Evaluation Type
- Criterion-referenced assessment: Measurement of skills compared to performance criterion
- Rating scales checklists: Others indicate occurrence or magnitude of behavior
- Self-report: Student indicates occurrence or magnitude of behavior

Learner Activities
- Listening to information presented verbally (lecture)
- Reading and writing
- Learning or self-management strategies
- Community activities
- Jobs
- Question/answer
- Videos
- Homework

Generalization
- Rehearsal of behavior to approximate real situations
- Practice in more than one setting
- Frequent review of skills or incorporated into new skills

5. Research and Field Testing

Research
- None reported

Field Testing
- Field test reported, but no outcome data presented

CHOICEMAKER SELF-DETERMINATION CURRICULUM: SELF-DIRECTED IEP

James E. Martin, Laura Huber Marshall, Laurie Maxson, and Patty Jerman

Sopris West, Inc.
4093 Specialty Place
Longmont, CO 80504
1-800-547-6747

Abstract

The *Self-Directed IEP* helps students learn the skills needed to actively participate in or even lead their own IEP staffings meeting. Students learn to express their interests, preferences, and limits and how to secure support to reach their own goals. Students learn valuable self-determination skills, including self-awareness, self-evaluation, goal setting, decision making, and cooperative meeting behaviors. The program includes two videotapes, a student workbook, a teacher's manual, and an assessment instrument. The "Self-Directed IEP in Action" video (7 minutes) introduces parents, students, and educators to the self-directed IEP process. The "Self-Directed IEP" video (17 minutes) models for students the 11 steps needed to lead their own IEP meeting. The teacher's manual provides supporting materials to prepare for successful implementation of the lessons, as well as overall instructional guidance. Included is the ChoiceMaker Self-Determination Assessment, which is a pre-post tool to measure student progress. This program is intended for students with mild to moderate learning disabilities, cognitive disabilities, and behavior problems, but it can be adapted for students with more severe disabilities.

1. Program Description

Type of Material

- Assessment tool
- Instructional tool

Students

- Noncategorical
- With mild or moderate learning disabilities or developmental disabilities
- Adaptations may be made for students who can't read or write

Ages

- Middle/junior high school
- Senior high school
- Adapted to upper elementary

Other

- Not specified

Self-Determination Content

- Self-awareness: Identifying information about self—interests, strengths, weaknesses
- Personal self-advocacy: Acting on one's knowledge of oneself and one's rights
- Goal setting: Deciding on desired outcomes
- Self-efficacy: Belief that one can accomplish one's goals
- Self-evaluation: Comparing one's performance to a standard
- Person-centered planning: Actively participating in planning activities such as planning one's own IEP
- Making choices and decisions
- Employment: Jobs, careers
- Education: Classes, sports, clubs, postsecondary education
- Housing and daily living: Home setting, daily living skills
- Personal: Recreation, leisure, legal, medical, health and wellness, relationships
- Community: Transportation, adult services, volunteering

2. Materials Description

Materials Provided

- Replicable worksheets or masters
- Consumable written materials
- Awareness-building video
- Instructional video
- Guide with background and overview
- Guide with directions for facilitating
- Other: Illustrations representing the crucial steps

Materials Packaging and Presentation

- Box

Equipment Needed

- VCR and monitor
- Overhead projector

Cost

- $120

3. Instructional Delivery

Setting

- Special education class
- Resource room

Instructional Grouping

- Not specified

Delivery Method

- Leader presents information
- Discovery/experiential: Participants complete activities related to objectives
- Group process: Participants interact with group members in activities related to objectives

Leader

- Not specified

Number of Leaders

- One

Leader Role

- Instructor: Leader-directed
- Facilitator: Facilitates group interaction

Leader Training

- Not specified

Lesson Sequence

- Set sequence

Frequency of Lesson Use

- Flexible

Required Preparation

- Make copies
- Make visual aids (flip charts, overheads, etc.)
- Other: Collect student's past IEPs

Number of Lessons

- IEP (11 lessons)

Lesson Time

- Average lesson time approximately 45 minutes each

4. Instructional Components

Objectives

- Objectives stated

Prerequisite Skills

- None identified

Quality of Instruction

- Targeted skills are clearly identified
- Skill sequence
- All activities align with objectives
- Examples used to teach concepts
- Cumulative review
- Spaced repetition
- Practice opportunities provided for targeted skills
- Modifications suggested for populations

Performance Evaluation Frequency

- Pretest and/or posttest
- Daily, weekly, or other regular assessment
- Long-term mastery

Performance Evaluation Type

- Criterion-referenced assessment: Measurement of skills compared to performance criterion
- Rating scales checklists: Others indicate occurrence or magnitude of behavior
- Self-report: Student indicates occurrence or magnitude of behavior
- Direct observation and recording: Observer uses measuring system to assess behavior as it occurs

Learner Activities

- Listening to information presented verbally (lecture)
- Reading and writing
- Group discussion
- Role play
- Question/answer
- Videos
- Learning or self-management strategies

Generalization

- Rehearsal of behavior to approximate real situations
- Practice rules for when to apply skills
- Frequent review of skills or incorporated into new skills
- Discussions of situations relevant to students in which they might use behavior
- Conditional discriminations taught

5. Research and Field Testing

Research

- Controlled studies
- Individual learner verification from assessment: Evaluation by learner outcomes

Field Testing

- Field test reported, but no outcome data presented

CHOICEMAKER SELF-DETERMINATION CURRICULUM: TAKE ACTION

Laura Huber Marshall, James E. Martin, Laurie Maxson, Terry L. Miller, Wanda Hughes, Toria McGill, and Patty Jerman

Sopris West, Inc.
4093 Specialty Place
Longmont, CO 80504
1-800-547-6747

Abstract

Take Action teaches students a generalizable process to attain their IEP and personal goals. A student instructional video and a sequence of seven lessons teach students the Take Action process. The "Take Action" video introduces the concept and shows how various students used the Take Action process to accomplish their goals. After establishing a goal, students answer the following six questions to develop their plan: (1) Standard: What will I be satisfied with? (2) Feedback: How will I get information on my performance? (3) Motivation: Why do I want to do this? (4) Strategy: What methods should I use? (5) Support: What help do I need? and (6) Schedule: When will I do it? After acting on their plan, students evaluate their plan and action and then make any necessary adjustments. The *Take Action* lessons were developed for all students—not just those with an IEP. Thus, the Take Action process may be used in general education academic and vocational environments, as well as in specialized learning settings. Included is the ChoiceMaker Self-Determination Assessment, which is a pre-post tool to measure student progress.

---

1. Program Description

Type of Material

- Assessment tool
- Instructional tool

Students

- Noncategorical
- Without disabilities

Ages

- Middle/junior high school
- Senior high school

Other

- Not specified

Self-Determination Content

- Self-efficacy: Belief that one can accomplish one's goals
- Goal setting: Deciding on desired outcomes
- Self-evaluation: Comparing one's performance to a standard
- Adjustment: Making adaptations to achieve desired outcomes
- Making choices and decisions
- Employment: Jobs, careers
- Education: Classes, sports, clubs, postsecondary education
- Housing and daily living: Home setting, daily living skills

- Personal: Recreation, leisure, legal, medical, health and wellness, relationships
- Community: Transportation, adult services, volunteering

2. Materials Description

Materials Provided

- Replicable worksheets or masters
- Instructional video
- Guide with background and overview
- Guide with directions for facilitating

Materials Packaging and Presentation

- Box

Equipment Needed

- VCR and monitor
- Overhead projector

Cost

- No information provided

3. Instructional Delivery

Setting

- General or special education class
- Resource or special education class

Instructional Grouping

- Large group (greater than 10)
- Small group (less than 10)

Delivery Method

- Leader presents information
- Discovery/experiential: Participants complete activities related to objectives
- Group process: Participants interact with group members in activities related to objectives

Leader

- Special educator
- General educator

Number of Leaders

- One

Leader Role

- Instructor: Leader-directed
- Facilitator: Facilitates group interaction

Leader Training

- Not specified

Lesson Sequence

- Set sequence

Frequency of Lesson Use

- Daily while learning the Take Action process
- Weekly after the process is learned and while it is being used

Required Preparation

- Make copies
- Make visual aids (flip charts, overheads, etc.)

Number of Lessons

- Seven

Lesson Time

- Average lesson time (45–50 minutes)

4. Instructional Components

Objectives

- Objectives stated

Prerequisite Skills

- None identified

Quality of Instruction

- Targeted skills are clearly identified
- Skill sequence
- All activities align with objectives
- Examples and nonexamples used to teach concepts
- Cumulative review
- Spaced repetition
- Practice opportunities provided for targeted skills
- Feedback procedures provided

Performance Evaluation Frequency

- Pretest and/or posttest
- Daily, weekly, or other regular assessment

Performance Evaluation Type

- Criterion-referenced assessment: Measurement of skills compared to performance criterion
- Self-report: Student indicates occurrence or magnitude of behavior
- Other (written assignments are completed during the lessons)

Learner Activities
- Listening to information presented verbally (lecture)
- Reading and writing
- Group discussion
- Question/answer
- Videos
- Learning or self-management strategies
- Homework

Generalization
- Rehearsal of behavior to approximate real situations

- Practice in more than one setting
- Practice rules for when to apply skills
- Conditional discriminations taught
- Frequent review of skills or incorporated into new skills

5. Research and Field Testing

Research
- Controlled study

Field Testing
- Field test reported, but no outcome data presented

COLORADO TRANSITION MANUAL

Susan McAlonan and Patricia A. Longo

Colorado Department of Education, Special Education Services Unit
201 East Colfax Avenue
Denver, CO 80203
303-866-6694

Abstract

The Colorado Transition Manual assists educators and service providers in developing a system to plan for transition from school to adult life for persons with disabilities. To accomplish this, a team of professionals and family members must be established and willing to institute creative solutions to complex problems. This manual provides information on the team process, planning, adult and community agencies involvement, student and family involvement, and the nature of instituting a change. A number of reproducible forms are provided.

1. Program Description

Type of Material
- Teacher/community information or training

Students
- Without disabilities
- Noncategorical

Ages
- Middle/junior high school
- Senior high school
- 18–21 years old

Other
- Educators
- Facilitators

Self-Determination Content
- Personal self-advocacy: Acting on one's knowledge of oneself and one's rights
- Goal setting: Deciding on desired outcomes
- Person-centered planning: Actively participating in planning activities such as planning one's own IEP
- Employment: Jobs, careers
- Education: Classes, sports, clubs, postsecondary education

- Housing and daily living: Home setting, daily living skills
- Personal: Recreation, leisure, legal, medical, health and wellness, relationships
- Community: Transportation, adult services, volunteering
- Systems design

2. Materials Description

Materials Provided
- Replicable worksheets or masters
- Guide with background and review

Materials Packaging and Presentation
- Three-ring notebooks

Equipment Needed
- Not specified

Cost
- $30

3. Instructional Delivery

Setting
- Not specified

Instructional Grouping
- Not specified

Delivery Method
- Not specified

Leader
- Not specified

Number of Leaders
- Not specified

Leader Role
- Not specified

Leader Training
- Not specified

Lesson Sequence
- Not specified

Frequency of Lesson Use
- Not specified

Required Preparation
- Not specified

Number of Lessons
- Not specified

Lesson Time
- Not specified

4. Instructional Components

Objectives
- Not specified

Prerequisite Skills
- Not specified

Quality of Instruction
- Not specified

Performance Evaluation Frequency
- Not specified

Performance Evaluation Type
- Not specified

Learner Activities
- Not specified

Generalization
- Not specified

5. Research and Field Testing

Research
- Not specified

Field Testing
- Not specified

CONNECTIONS: A TRANSITION CURRICULUM FOR GRADES 3 THROUGH 6

Art Aspinall, Lynn Roberts, and Ruth Robinson
Colorado Department of Education
201 East Colfax Avenue
Denver, CO 80203
303-866-6694

Abstract

This curriculum provides an equal balance between several concepts, including career awareness; attitudes, values, and habits; human relationships; occupational information; and acquisition of job and daily living skills. Its purpose is to impact work personalities early on in the school years through teaching crucial career education and self-determination concepts. Self-determination is not directly addressed, but many self-determination concepts are discussed. Emphasized in three units are career development, career orientation, and career exploration. Unit 1, "Me and My Shadow," introduces the self-determination skills of self-awareness and goal setting through sections on "getting to know me," "positive self-esteem," and "goal setting." The other two units present typical career development concepts.

1. Program Description

Type of Material
- Instructional tool

Students
- Without disabilities
- Noncategorical
- At risk

Ages
- Elementary school (grades 3–6)
- Middle/junior high school

Other
- Not specified

Self-Determination Content
- Self-awareness: Identifying information about self—interests, strengths, weaknesses
- Personal self-advocacy: Acting on one's knowledge of oneself and one's rights
- Goal setting: Deciding on desired outcomes
- Self-evaluation: Comparing one's performance to a standard
- Person-centered planning: Actively participating in planning activities such as planning one's own IEP
- Employment: Jobs, careers
- Education: Classes, sports, clubs, postsecondary education
- Housing and daily living: Home setting, daily living skills
- Personal: Recreation, leisure, legal, medical, health and wellness, relationships
- Community: Transportation, adult services, volunteering
- Conflict resolution and problem solving
- Making choices and decisions

2. Materials Description

Materials Provided
- Replicable worksheets or masters
- Instructional video
- Guide with background and overview
- Guide with directions for facilitating

Materials Packaging and Presentation
- Loose pages

Equipment Needed
- Overhead projector

Cost
- Less than $100

3. Instructional Delivery

Setting

- Not specified

Instructional Grouping

- Not specified

Delivery Method

- Leader presents information
- Discovery/experiential: Participants complete activities related to objectives
- Group process: Participants interact with group members in activities related to objectives
- Community-based instruction: Experiences in the community

Leader

- Not specified

Number of Leaders

- One or two depending on group size

Leader Role

- Not specified

Leader Training

- Not specified

Lesson Sequence

- Flexible sequence

Frequency of Lesson Use

- Flexible

Required Preparation

- Make copies
- Make visual aids (flip charts, overheads, etc.)
- Schedule guest speakers
- Secure community sites
- Other: Make supplies

Number of Lessons

- Not specified

Lesson Time

- Not specified

4. Instructional Components

Objectives

- Objectives stated

Prerequisite Skills

- None identified

Quality of Instruction

- Targeted skills are clearly identified
- Skill sequence
- All activities align with objectives
- Examples and nonexamples used to teach concepts
- Practice opportunities provided for targeted skills
- Modifications suggested for populations

Performance Evaluation Frequency

- Pretest and/or posttest
- Long-term mastery assessment

Performance Evaluation Type

- Self-report: Student indicates occurrence or magnitude of behavior

Learner Activities

- Listening to information presented verbally (lecture)
- Reading and writing
- Group discussion
- Role play
- Games
- Community activities
- Question/answer
- Volunteering
- Homework
- Learning or self-management strategies
- Jobs

Generalization

- Rehearsal of behavior to approximate real situations
- Practice in more than one setting
- Discussions of situations relevant to students in which they might use behavior

5. Research and Field Testing

Research

- None reported

Field Testing

- Field test reported, but no outcome data presented

FOSTERING SELF-DETERMINATION: Activities, Resources, Lessons, and Video

Kathy Ben, Christine M. Andersen, and James Wiedle
Center for Human Development, University of Alaska Affiliated Program
Self-Determination Project
2330 Nicholas Street
Anchorage, AK 99508

Abstract

The materials contained in *Fostering Self-Determination* are a compilation of activities and lesson plans from numerous resources. The goal for this guide is to provide educators with a basic understanding of the concept of self-determination and to present a wide variety of sample lessons and curricula designed to enhance self-determination skills. The Guide presents the following topics as important elements of self-determination: (a) self-awareness; (b) interpersonal communications; (c) assertiveness; (d) goal setting; (e) creative problem solving; (f) video-based personal future planning; and (g) video self-modeling. A brief introduction opens each section, followed by lessons and activities designed to address that particular area of need. A companion video, "Fostering Self-Determination," shows how the various strategies can be used to increase self-determination skills.

1. Program Description

Type of Material

- Instructional tool

Students

- Not specified

Ages

- Not specified

Other

- Not specified

Self-Determination Content

- Self-awareness: Identifying information about self—interests, strengths, weaknesses
- Personal self-advocacy: Acting on one's knowledge of oneself and one's rights
- Goal setting: Deciding on desired outcomes
- Self-evaluation: Comparing one's performance to a standard
- Person-centered planning: Actively participating in planning activities such as planning one's own IEP
- Making choices and decisions
- Employment: Jobs, careers
- Personal: Recreation, leisure, legal, medical, health and wellness, relationships

2. Materials Description

Materials Provided

- Replicable worksheets or masters
- Awareness-building video
- Guide with background and review
- Guide with directions for facilitating

Materials Packaging and Presentation

- Spiral bound

Equipment Needed

- Overhead projector
- Flip chart
- VCR and monitor

Cost

- No information provided

3. Instructional Delivery

Setting
- Not specified

Instructional Grouping
- Not specified

Delivery Method
- Leader presents information
- Discovery/experiential: Participants complete activities related to objectives
- Group process: Participants interact with group members in activities related to objectives

Leader
- Not specified

Number of Leaders
- Not specified

Leader Role
- Instructor: Leader directed
- Facilitator: Facilitates group interaction
- Coparticipant/colearner: participates with group

Leader Training
- Not specified

Lesson Sequence
- Not specified

Frequency of Lesson Use
- Not specified

Required Preparation
- Make copies
- Make visual aids (flip charts, overheads, etc.)
- Secure community sites
- Collect materials for projects

Number of Lessons
- Not specified

Lesson Time
- Not specified

4. Instructional Components

Objectives
- Objectives stated

Prerequisite Skills
- Not identified

Quality of Instruction
- Targeted skills are clearly identified
- All activities align with objectives
- Examples and nonexamples used to teach concepts
- Practice opportunities provided for targeted skills

Performance Evaluation Frequency
- None

Performance Evaluation Type
- Videotaping for self-review

Learner Activities
- Listening to information presented verbally (lecture)
- Reading and writing
- Group discussion
- Role play
- Games
- Community activities
- Question/answer
- Videos
- Learning or self-management strategies

Generalization
- Rehearsal of behavior to approximate real situations
- Practice in more than one setting
- Discussions of situations relevant to students in which they might use behavior

5. Research and Field Testing

Research
- User feedback: Users provide feedback on value of program

Field Testing
- Not reported

GROUP ACTION PLANNING: AN INNOVATIVE MANUAL FOR BUILDING A SELF-DETERMINED FUTURE

Emma Longan Anderson, Kimberly Seaton, Patricia Dinas, and Arthur Satterfield

Full Citizenship, Inc.
211 East 8th Street, Suite F
Lawrence, KS 66044
913-749-0603

Abstract

The goal of the *Group Action Planning* manual is to provide a blueprint for helping students reach their goals, make decisions, acquire needed supports, and secure a self-determined future. The group action procedures are designed to be taught to students through a semester-long class. A construction theme is used to present the information. The sections of the manual are (1) "Group Action Planning Blueprint" (what the group is and who the key players are); (2) "Ground Breaking" (facilitation rules, interests, strengths, and needs); (3) "Laying Foundation" (goal setting and envisioning); (4) "Building Bridges" (decision making and conflict resolution); (5) "Potholes and Road Construction" (loss of focus and dispersed activity); (6) "Dedication Ceremonies" (celebrating accomplishments); and (7) "Resources." Each section begins with case study examples, then provides tips on how to teach that section. Samples are included in each instructional section.

1. Program Description

Type of Material

- Instructional tool

Students

- Not specified

Ages

- Not specified

Other

- Mentors

Self-Determination Content

- Goal setting: Deciding on desired outcomes
- Person-centered planning: Actively participating in planning activities such as planning one's own IEP
- Making choices and decisions
- Employment: Jobs, careers
- Education: Classes, sports, clubs, postsecondary education
- Housing and daily living: Home setting, daily living skills
- Personal: Recreation, leisure, legal, medical, health and wellness, relationships
- Community: Transportation, adult services, volunteering

2. Materials Description

Materials Provided

- Guide with background and overview
- Guide with directions for facilitating

Materials Packaging and Presentation

- Three-ring binder

Equipment Needed

- Not specified

Cost

- Less than $100

3. Instructional Delivery

Setting
- Not specified

Instructional Grouping
- Small group: Less than 10

Delivery Method
- Group process: Participants interact with group members in activities related to objectives

Leader
- Other: Facilitator

Number of Leaders
- One

Leader Role
- Facilitator: Facilitates group interaction

Leader Training
- Not specified

Lesson Sequence
- Set sequence

Frequency of Lesson Use
- Not specified

Required Preparation
- Other: Schedule meetings

Number of Lessons
- Six major sections

Lesson Time
- No information provided

4. Instructional Components

Objectives
- Not specified

Prerequisite Skills
- None identified

Quality of Instruction
- Examples used to teach concepts

Performance Evaluation Frequency
- None mentioned

Performance Evaluation Type
- None

Learner Activities
- Group discussion
- Listening to information presented verbally (lecture)—assumed to occur

Generalization
- No procedures mentioned

5. Research and Field Testing

Research
- User feedback: Users provide feedback on value of program

Field Testing
- Not reported

IN THEIR OWN WORDS Video and Study Guide

Terence Collins, Lynda Price, Sheryl Evelo, Janis Johnson, and David Shroat

General College, University of Minnesota
140 Appleby Hall
128 Pleasant St., S.E.
Minneapolis, MN 55455
612-625-5366

Abstract

The goal of the *In Their Own Words* lesson package is to help teachers, students, families, and adult providers to increase their awareness of the secondary-to-adult-world transition process. *In Their Own Words* consists of a video and supporting materials. The video shows an interview with five former special education students who all made successful transitions from high school to a postsecondary educational setting. Each individual in the video describes the transition experience in his or her own words. During the interviews the students described themselves and the preparation and experiences in high school and at their postsecondary educational setting. The video is structured with several built-in pauses during which students may discuss the issues just raised. The Study Guide provides suggestions for topics that can be discussed during these pauses. The Study Guide also includes a detailed biography of each of the five students interviewed on the video, along with supplemental resources.

1. Program Description

Type of Material

- Instructional tool

Students

- Not specified
- With mild or moderate behavioral or emotional disabilities

Ages

- Senior high school
- 18–21 years old

Other

- Families
- Educators
- Facilitators
- Other professionals

Self-Determination Content

- Self-awareness: Identifying information about self—interests, strengths, weaknesses
- Personal self-advocacy: Acting on one's knowledge of oneself and one's rights
- Employment: Jobs, careers
- Education: Classes, sports, clubs, postsecondary education
- Community: Transportation, adult services, volunteering

2. Materials Description

Materials Provided

- Awareness-building video
- Overheads
- Computer software
- Guide with background and review
- Guide with directions for facilitating

Materials Packaging and Presentation

- Spiral bound

Equipment Needed

- Overhead projector
- VCR and monitor

Cost

- No information provided

3. Instructional Delivery

Setting

- Not specified

Instructional Grouping

- Not specified

Delivery Method

- Group process: Participants interact with group members in activities related to objectives

Leader

- Not specified

Number of Leaders

- Not specified

Leader Role

- Facilitator: Facilitates group interaction

Leader Training

- Not specified

Lesson Sequence

- Flexible sequence

Frequency of Lesson Use
- Not specified

Required Preparation
- Not specified

Number of Lessons
- Not specified

Lesson Time
- Not specified

4. Instructional Components

Objectives
- Not specified

Prerequisite Skills
- None identified

Quality of Instruction
- None of the indicators mentioned in the materials

Performance Evaluation Frequency
- None

Performance Evaluation Type
- None

Learner Activities
- Group discussion
- Role play
- Question/answer
- Videos

Generalization
- None provided

5. Research and Field Testing

Research
- None provided

Field Testing
- None

IRVINE UNIFIED SCHOOL DISTRICT SELF-DETERMINATION MATERIALS: STUDENT STRATEGIES, SUPPORT STRATEGIES, AND TRANSITION

Marilyn Tabor, Diane Deboer, and Linda O'Neal
Horizons Program
Irvine Unified School District
5050 Barranca Parkway
Irvine, CA 92714-4698
714-651-0444

Abstract

Three different sets of materials comprise the package: (1) *Transition: A Handbook for Parents, Students, and Advocates*; (2) *Interventions: A System Guide*; and (3) *Student Strategies: A Coaching Guide*. The *Student Strategy* book is available only from the California Department of Education and is accompanied by a training audiotape. The other materials are available from the Irvine Unified School District. The *Transition* manual is a fact book covering topics such as transition, legal issues, funding issues, and support services—much of which is targeted for California. *Interventions: A System Guide* describes the system effort that supports the *Student Strategies* curriculum. Included are sections that describe the mentor, parent, and collaboration components. The *Student Strategies* manual provides detailed instruction in eight areas, including goal setting, information gathering, planning, decision making, problem solving, communication, self-advocacy, and coping/self-talk. Coaching is emphasized throughout the manual as the main approach to help the student define and construct a personal approach to becoming self-determined.

1. Program Description

Type of Material

- Instructional tool
- Assessment tool

Students

- Without disabilities, noncategorical, at risk
- With mild or moderate learning disabilities or developmental disabilities
- With mild or moderate behavioral or emotional disabilities

Ages

- Senior high school

Other

- Families
- Other professionals

Self-Determination Content

- Self-awareness: Identifying information about self—interests, strengths, weaknesses
- Personal self-advocacy: Acting on one's knowledge of oneself and one's rights
- Goal setting: Deciding on desired outcomes
- Self-evaluation: Comparing one's performance to a standard
- Making choices and decisions
- Employment: Jobs, careers
- Education: Classes, sports, clubs, postsecondary education
- Community: Transportation, adult services, volunteering
- Housing and daily living: Home setting, daily living skills
- Personal: Recreation, leisure, legal, medical, health and wellness, relationships
- System self-advocacy: Taking action to change systems

2. Materials Description

Materials Provided

- Replicable worksheets or masters
- Guide with background and overview
- Guide with directions for facilitating
- Audio materials

Materials Packaging and Presentation

- Three-ring binders *Systems* and *Student*
- Book for *Transitions*

Equipment Needed

- Overhead projector

Cost

- Between $100 and $200 (for all three books and tape)

3. Instructional Delivery

Setting

- Not specified

Instructional Grouping

- Small groups (less than 10)
- Individual (one-to-one tutoring)

Delivery Method

- Leader presents information
- Discovery/experiential: Participants complete activities related to objectives
- Group process: Participants interact with group members in activities related to objectives
- Community-based instruction: Experiences in the community

Leader

- Special educator
- Support personnel
- Parent

Number of Leaders

- One

Leader Role

- Facilitator: Facilitates group interaction
- Instructor: Leader directed

Leader Training

- Specific pretraining required: Listen to audiotape

Lesson Sequence
- Set sequence

Frequency of Lesson Use
- Weekly

Required Preparation
- Make copies
- Make visual aids (flip charts, over-heads, etc.)
- Create examples
- Schedule and/or train mentors
- Gather community information and order other curricular materials

Number of Lessons
- 30

Lesson Time
- 50 minutes

4. Instructional Components

Objectives
- Objectives stated
- Objectives measurable—observable behavior, conditions, criteria

Prerequisite Skills
- None

Quality of Instruction
- Targeted skills are clearly identified
- Examples and nonexamples used to teach concepts
- All activities align with objectives
- Spaced repetition
- Practice opportunities provided for targeted skills
- Feedback procedures provided

Performance Evaluation Frequency
- Other: Cumulative portfolio

Performance Evaluation Type
- Criterion-referenced assessment: Measurement of skills compared to performance criterion
- Self-report: Student indicates occurrence or magnitude of behavior

Learner Activities
- Listening to information presented verbally (lecture)
- Reading and writing
- Group discussion
- Role play
- Question/answer
- Mentoring
- Learning or self-management strategies

Generalization
- Rehearsal of behavior to approximate real situations
- Practice in more than one setting
- Practice rules for when to apply skills
- Frequent review of skills or incorporated into new skills
- Discussions of situations relevant to students in which they might use behavior
- Conditional discriminations taught

5. Research and Field Testing

Research
- User feedback: Users provide feedback on value of program
- Expert appraisal: Material given appraisal by area experts

Field Testing
- Field test reported, but no outcome data presented

LEARNING WITH PURPOSE: AN INSTRUCTOR'S MANUAL FOR TEACHING SELF-DETERMINATION SKILLS TO STUDENTS WHO ARE AT-RISK FOR FAILURE

Loretta A. Serna and JoAnne Lau-Smith

University of New Mexico
College of Education 215
Albuquerque, NM 87131
505-277-5119

Abstract

Learning with Purpose is a comprehensive self-determination curriculum designed for students with mild and moderate disabilities and students who are at risk for failure in home, school, and community environments. The program is appropriate for students between the ages of 13 and 25 years. Self-evaluation, self-direction, networking, collaboration, persistence and risk taking, and dealing with stress comprise the self-determination skills that are systematically taught in this program. Students clearly define the skill, understand how the skill will be useful to them, rehearse the skill, evaluate their own performance, reach skill mastery, and participate in activities that will help them use their skills in a variety of environments. A corresponding parent program accompanies this curriculum, and many parents may learn how to support students while they acquire new skills.

1. Program Description

Type of Material
- Instructional tool
- Assessment tool

Students
- At risk and those without disabilities
- With mild or moderate learning disabilities or developmental disabilities
- With mild or moderate behavioral or emotional disabilities

Ages
- Middle/junior high school
- Senior high school
- 18–21 years old and older

Other
- Not specified

Self-Determination Content
- Self-awareness: Identifying information about self—interests, strengths, weaknesses
- Personal self-advocacy: Acting on one's knowledge of oneself and one's rights
- Self-efficacy: Belief that one can accomplish one's goals
- Goal setting: Deciding on desired outcomes
- Self-evaluation: Comparing one's performance to a standard
- Adjustment: Making adaptations to achieve desired outcomes
- Making choices and decisions

2. Materials Description

Materials Provided
- Replicable worksheets or masters
- Consumable written materials
- Guide with background and review
- Guide with directions for facilitating

Materials Packaging and Presentation
- Three-ring binder

Equipment Needed
- Overhead projector

Cost
- No information provided

3. Instructional Delivery

Setting
- General education class
- Community and other service agencies such as counseling service

Instructional Grouping

- Not specified

Delivery Method

- Leader presents information
- Discovery/experiential: Participants complete activities related to objectives

Leader

- Not specified

Number of Leaders

- Not specified

Leader Role

- Instructor: Presents information
- Facilitator: Facilitates group interaction
- Model: Demonstrates process

Leader Training

- Specific pretraining required: Must complete training to secure materials

Lesson Sequence

- Flexible sequence

Frequency of Lesson Use

- Flexible: Takes 2–4 years to complete all lessons

Required Preparation

- Not specified

Number of Lessons

- 34

Lesson Time

- One to two 45-minute sessions

4. Instructional Components

Objectives

- Objectives stated

Prerequisite Skills

- Listed
- Assessment guidelines provided

Quality of Instruction

- Targeted skills are clearly identified
- Skill sequence
- All activities align with objectives
- Examples used to teach concepts
- Practice opportunities provided for targeted skills

- Feedback procedures provided
- Remedial procedures provided
- Modifications suggested for populations

Performance Evaluation Frequency

- Pretest and/or posttest
- Daily, weekly, or other regular assessment

Performance Evaluation Type

- Criterion-referenced assessment: Measurement of skills compared to performance criterion
- Rating scales checklists: Others indicate occurrence or magnitude of behavior
- Self-report: Student indicates occurrence or magnitude of behavior
- Direct observation and recording: Observer uses measuring system to assess behavior as it occurs

Learner Activities

- Listening to information presented verbally (lecture)
- Reading and writing
- Group discussion
- Role play
- Community activities
- Question/answer
- Homework
- Learning or self-management strategies

Generalization

- Rehearsal of behavior to approximate real situations
- Practice in more than one setting
- Conditional discriminations taught
- Frequent review of skills or incorporated into new skills
- Discussions of situations relevant to students in which they might use behavior

5. Research and Field Testing

Research

- Expert appraisal: Material given appraisal by area experts
- User feedback: Users provide feedback on value of program

Field Testing

- None reported

LESSONS FOR LIVING: A SELF-DETERMINATION CURRICULUM FOR TRANSITIONAL AGED STUDENTS

Wendy Kurland, Jennifer Rush Simms, Karen Hampton Young, and Ruthie-Marie Beckwith

Janes Stanfield Co., Inc.
Drawer 125
P.O. Box 41058
Santa Barbara, CA 93140
1-800-431-6534

Abstract

A group of adults with disabilities who spent time with secondary-age students who visited their People First chapter realized the need for younger people to learn about self-advocacy and self-determination. From this idea, the People First group in Tennessee wrote *Lessons for Living* to show how People First clubs could organize and operate in high schools, just like any other high school activity club for students with or without disabilities. This lesson package provides detailed activities to help students develop leadership, meeting, decision-making, and planning skills to empower youth to speak for themselves. Two complementary sets of lessons provide detailed activity suggestions to teach 20 different skills, including how to introduce self to others, how to get needed information, and how to ignore positive and negative coercion.

1. Program Description

Type of Material

- Instructional tool

Students

- Without disabilities
- With mild or moderate behavioral or emotional disabilities

Ages

- Senior high school

Other

- Families

Self-Determination Content

- Self-awareness: Identifying information about self—interests, strengths, weaknesses
- Personal self-advocacy: Acting on one's knowledge of oneself and one's rights
- System self-advocacy: Taking action to change systems
- Goal setting: Deciding on desired outcomes
- Self-evaluation: Comparing one's performance to a standard
- Person-centered planning: Student actively participating in planning activities such as planning one's own IEP
- Making choices and decisions
- Employment: Jobs, careers
- Education: Classes, sports, clubs, postsecondary education
- Housing and daily living: Home setting, daily living skills
- Community: Transportation, adult services, volunteering

2. Materials Description

Materials Provided

- Replicable worksheets or masters
- Guide with background and overview
- Guide with directions for facilitating
- Games
- Activity cards

Materials Packaging and Presentation
- Three-ring binder

Equipment Needed
- VCR and monitor
- Camcorder

Cost
- Less than $100

3. Instructional Delivery

Setting
- After-school activity (extra curricula or evening activity)

Instructional Grouping
- Not specified

Delivery Method
- Leader presents information
- Discovery/experiential: Participants complete activities related to objectives
- Group process: Participants interact with group members in activities related to objectives
- Community-based instruction

Leader
- Special educator, general educator, support personnel, parent, advisor, or individual with a disability

Number of Leaders
- Not specified

Leader Role
- Instructor: Presents information
- Facilitator: Facilitates group interaction
- Coparticipant/colearner

Leader Training
- Not specified

Lesson Sequence
- Not specified

Frequency of Lesson Use
- Not specified

Required Preparation
- Not specified

Number of Lessons
- 40 (in two sets of complementary lessons)

Lesson Time
- 10–30 minutes

4. Instructional Components

Objectives
- Objectives stated

Prerequisite Skills
- Not specified

Quality of Instruction
- Modifications suggested for populations
- Practice opportunities provided for target skills

Performance Evaluation Frequency
- Not specified

Performance Evaluation Type
- Not specified

Learner Activities
- Listening to information presented verbally (lecture)
- Reading and writing
- Group discussion
- Role play
- Community activities
- Question/answer
- Games
- Videos
- Mentoring
- Volunteering
- Homework

Generalization
- None reported

5. Research and Field Testing

Research
- User feedback: Users provide feedback on value of program

Field Testing
- None reported

LIFE CENTERED CAREER EDUCATION

Donn E. Brolin

The Council for Exceptional Children
1920 Association Drive
Reston, VA 20191-1589
888-232-7323

Abstract

Life Centered Career Education is a comprehensive career education curriculum and lesson plan package designed to teach special education and other at risk populations the skills to function successfully as productive workers in their homes and communities. The LCCE complete package includes three domains (daily living skills, personal-social skills, and occupational guidance and preparation), 20 competency areas, and 97 subcompetencies. Self-determination concepts are infused throughout the curriculum. Included in the complete package are Competency Assessment Knowledge Batteries and Performance Batteries, teacher instructional materials, and a 175-page guide, *Life Centered Career Education: A Competency Based Approach.*

1. Program Description

Type of Material

- Assessment tool
- Instructional tool

Students

- Noncategorical
- At risk

Ages

- Middle/junior high school
- Senior high school
- 18–21 years old

Other

- Adults

Self-Determination Content

- Self-awareness: Identifying information about self—interests, strengths, weaknesses
- Personal self-advocacy: Acting on one's knowledge of oneself and one's rights
- Goal setting: Deciding on desired outcomes
- Making choices and decisions

- Employment: Jobs, careers
- Education: Classes, sports, clubs, postsecondary education
- Housing and daily living: Home setting, daily living skills
- Personal: Recreation, leisure, legal, medical, health and wellness, relationships
- Community: Transportation, adult services, volunteering

2. Materials Description

Materials Provided

- Replicable worksheets or masters
- Games
- Guide with background and overview
- Guide with directions for facilitating

Materials Packaging and Presentation

- Ten three-ring binders

Equipment Needed

- Art supplies

Cost

- $980

3. Instructional Delivery

Setting
- General education class
- Special education class
- Resource room

Instructional Grouping
- Not specified

Delivery Method
- Leader presents information
- Discovery/experiential: Participants complete activities related to objectives
- Group process: Participants interact with group members in activities related to objectives

Leader
- Not specified

Number of Leaders
- Not specified

Leader Role
- Instructor: Presents information
- Facilitator: Facilitates group interaction
- Model: Demonstrates process

Leader Training
- Available through The Council for Exceptional Children

Participation Requirements
- Not specified

Lesson Sequence
- Flexible sequence

Frequency of Lesson Use
- Not specified

Required Preparation
- Make visual aids (flip charts, overheads, etc.)
- Make copies
- Create examples
- Schedule guest speakers
- Gather community information

Number of Lessons
- Over 1,100 in all

- Approximately 350 self-determination related

Lesson Time
- Not specified

4. Instructional Components

Objectives
- Objectives stated
- Objectives measurable: Observable behavior, conditions, criteria

Prerequisite Skills
- Assessment guidelines provided

Quality of Instruction
- Targeted skills are clearly identified
- Skill sequence
- All activities align with objectives
- Examples used to teach concepts
- Spaced repetition
- Practice opportunities provided for targeted skills
- Feedback procedures provided
- Remedial procedures provided
- Modifications suggested for populations

Performance Evaluation Frequency
- Pretest and/or posttest
- Daily, weekly, or other regular assessment

Performance Evaluation Type
- Rating scales checklists: Others indicate occurrence or magnitude of behavior
- Knowledge batteries
- Performance batteries
- Self-report: Student indicates occurrence or magnitude of behavior

Learner Activities
- Listening to information presented verbally (lecture)
- Reading and writing
- Group discussion
- Role play
- Games
- Community activities
- Jobs
- Question/answer

Generalization

- Rehearsal of behavior to approximate real situations
- Practice in more than one setting
- Conditional discriminations taught (when to apply rules, examples, and nonexamples)
- Frequent review of skills or incorporated into new skills
- Discussions of situations relevant to students in which they might use behavior

5. Research and Field Testing

Research

- Expert appraisal: Material given appraisal by area experts

Field Testing

- Publisher testimonials: Publisher describes value of program
- One group field tests (pre- and posttest): Evaluation of materials reported with regard to user group performance on objectives without control group; data included

---

NEXT S.T.E.P.

A. S. Halpern, C. M. Herr, N. K. Wolf, J. E. Lawson, B. Doren, and M. C. Johnson

Pro-Ed Publishing Company
8700 Shoal Creek Boulevard
Austin, TX 78757-6897
512/451-3246

Abstract

The *Next S.T.E.P.* curriculum is designed to help adolescents—both those with and those without disabilities—learn how to do transition planning. The lessons are structured to help students become motivated to engage in transition planning, engage in meaningful and useful self-evaluation, identify and select feasible and personally desired transition goals and activities, and take responsibility for conducting their own transition planning when needed. The *Next S.T.E.P.* curriculum consists of 19 lessons, most of which can be delivered in 50-minute class periods. The curriculum materials include (a) a teacher's manual that contains lesson plans and black line masters for overhead transparencies as well as guidelines for involving parents or other family members in the student's transition process; (b) student workbooks that include worksheets used in the lessons and plan sheets and other forms that students will need to produce their transition plans; and (c) an entertaining and instructive video with a number of vignettes that play a motivational and instructional role in several of the lessons. The *Next S.T.E.P.* curriculum has been field tested with more than 1,000 students and their families.

1. Program Description

Type of Material
- Instructional tool
- Assessment tool

Students
- Without disabilities
- Noncategorical
- At risk

Ages
- Senior high school
- 18–21 years old

Other
- Families

Self-Determination Content
- Self-awareness: Identifying information about self—interests, strengths, weaknesses
- Self-efficacy: Belief that one can accomplish one's goals
- Goal setting: Deciding on desired outcomes
- Self-evaluation: Comparing one's performance to a standard
- Adjustment: Making adaptations to achieve desired outcomes
- Person-centered planning: Student actively participating in planning activities such as planning one's own IEP
- Making choices and decisions
- Employment: Jobs, careers
- Education: Classes, sports, clubs, postsecondary education
- Housing and daily living: Home setting, daily living skills
- Community: Transportation, adult services, volunteering

2. Materials Description

Materials Provided
- Replicable worksheets or masters
- Consumable written materials
- Awareness building video
- Instructional video
- Activity cards
- Games
- Guide with background and overview
- Guide with directions for facilitating

Materials Packaging and Presentation
- Spiral bound

Equipment Needed
- Overhead projector
- VCR and monitor

Cost
- Between $100 and $200

3. Instructional Delivery

Setting
- General education class/infused into existing classes
- Special education, including resource room

Instructional Grouping
- Large and small groups
- Individual (one-to-one tutoring)

Delivery Method
- Leader presents information
- Discovery/experiential: Participants complete activities related to objectives
- Group process: Participants interact with group members in activities related to objectives
- Community-based instruction: Experiences in the community

Leader
- Special educator
- General educator

Number of Leaders
- One

Leader Role
- Instructor: Leader directed
- Facilitator: Facilitates group interaction
- Model: Demonstrates process

Leader Training
- Not specified

Lesson Sequence
- Set sequence

Frequency of Lesson Use
- Several times per week

Required Preparation
- Make visual aids (flip charts, overheads, etc.)
- Read lesson plans

Number of Lessons
- 19

Lesson Time
- 50 minutes

4. Instructional Components

Objectives
- Objectives stated
- Objectives measurable—observable behavior, conditions, criteria

Prerequisite Skills
- None specified

Quality of Instruction
- Targeted skills are clearly identified
- Skill sequence
- All activities align with objectives
- Cumulative review
- Spaced repetition
- Modifications suggested for populations
- Examples used to teach concepts
- Practice opportunities provided for targeted skills
- Feedback procedures provided
- Remedial procedures provided

Performance Evaluation Frequency
- Daily, weekly, or other regular assessment

Performance Evaluation Type
- Rating scales checklists: Others indicatee occurrence or magnitude of behavior
- Self-report: Student indicates occurrence or magnitude of behavior
- Other: Parent and teacher inventories

Learner Activities
- Listening to information presented verbally (lecture)
- Reading and writing
- Group discussion
- Games
- Question/answer
- Videos
- Role play
- Jobs
- Homework
- Learning or self-management strategies

Generalization
- Rehearsal of behavior to approximate real situations
- Practice rules for when to apply skills
- Frequent review of skills or incorporated into new skills
- Discussions of situations relevant to students in which they might use behavior

5. Research and Field Testing

Research
- User feedback: Users provide feedback on value of program

Field Testing
- Field test reported, but no outcome data presented (over 1,000 students)

PROJECT PARTNERSHIP: A MODEL PROGRAM FOR ENCOURAGING SELF-DETERMINATION THROUGH ACCESS TO THE ARTS

Very Special Arts
1331 F Street, N.W., Suite 800
Washington, DC 20004
202-628-8080

Abstract

This Instructional Kit is designed to use the arts as a means to teach students with disabilities self-determination skills. Through a three-step framework, students explore ways to take control of their own lives, advocate for themselves, make choices, set goals, and take steps to achieve them. The three steps are (1) activity mapping, (2) student review of the art activity, and (3) a partnership group. Included is a site assessment process to identify barriers to participation by students with disabilities in the arts and different student forms to help plan and self-assess. Activity suggestions are provided across drama, dance, music, creative writing, and photography and other visual arts. Included is an awareness-building video that shows various accomplished artists—all of whom have disabilities—talking about why self-determination is important in their lives.

1. Program Description

Type of Material

- Instructional tool
- Assessment tool

Students

- Not specified

Ages

- Senior high school

Other

- Not specified

Self-Determination Content

- Self-awareness: Identifying information about self—interests, strengths, weaknesses
- Adjustment: Making adaptations to achieve desired outcomes
- Goal setting: Deciding on desired outcomes
- Self-evaluation: Comparing one's performance to a standard
- Making choices and decisions
- Employment: Jobs, careers
- Personal: Recreation, leisure, legal, medical, health and wellness, relationships

2. Materials Description

Materials Provided

- Guide with background and review
- Guide with directions for facilitating
- Other (many art lesson ideas)
- Awareness-building video that shows various artists talking about self-determination

Materials Packaging and Presentation

- Three-ring binder

Equipment Needed

- VCR and monitor
- Other—art supplies

Cost

- No information provided

3. Instructional Delivery

Setting

- Art class or other similar location
- After-school activity (e.g., extra-curricular or evening activities)

Instructional Grouping

- Not specified

Delivery Method

- Leader presents information
- Discovery/experiential: Participants complete activities related to objectives
- Group process: Participants interact with group members in activities related to objectives

Leader

- Special educator
- Other—art teacher

Number of Leaders

- Two (special educator and art teacher)

Leader Role

- Instructor: Leader directed
- Facilitator: Facilitates group interaction
- Model: Demonstrates process

Leader Training

- Not specified

Lesson Sequence

- Not specified

Frequency of Lesson Use

- Not specified

Required Preparation

- Other (get filmstrip and art supplies)
- Create examples
- Order other curricular materials
- Other (gather materials, props, and art supplies)

Number of Lessons

- 20–40

Lesson Time

- 50 minutes

4. Instructional Components

Objectives

- Objectives stated

Prerequisite Skills

- None identified

Quality of Instruction

- Targeted skills are clearly identified
- All activities align with objectives
- Spaced repetition
- Feedback procedures provided
- Modifications suggested for populations
- Examples and non-examples used to teach concepts

Performance Evaluation Frequency

- Daily, weekly, or other regular assessment

Performance Evaluation Type

- Self-report: Student indicates occurrence or magnitude of behavior
- Other: Parent and teacher inventories

Learner Activities

- Listening to information presented verbally (lecture)
- Group discussion
- Reading and writing
- Role play
- Other: Music, dance, sculpture, drawing, etc.

Generalization

- Rehearsal of behavior to approximate real situations

5. Research and Field Testing

Research

- None reported

Field Testing

- Field test reported, but no outcome data presented—two schools

"PUTTING FEET ON MY DREAMS": A PROGRAM IN SELF-DETERMINATION FOR ADOLESCENTS AND YOUNG ADULTS

Ann Fullerton

Department of Special and Counselor Education
Portland State University
P.O. Box 751
Portland, OR 97207-0751

Abstract

This curriculum provides students opportunities to explore self-determination through (a) learning from each other and their teachers; (b) a variety of experiential, self-assessment, and student-directed learning activities; and (c) building a self-folio. The basic premise is that students need both life and self-knowledge along with life planning in order to be self-determined. The curriculum is stand alone, but it was designed to provide a framework in which to make self-determination the overall theme that ties together one's life skills and vocational and other programs. The curriculum contains seven units such as life planning, in which students develop and implement personal goals. Unique to this curriculum are detailed units in the areas of communication, learning, and organization. The purpose of the communication unit is to increase student's awareness of being an effective communicator, examine verbal and nonverbal actions, and self-assess communication skills. The purpose of the learning unit is to become aware of how one uses visual and auditory information to learn and remember and general learning strategies. The purpose of the unit on organization is to understand the relationship between self-organization and independence and to learn strategies for organizing tasks, time, and materials.

1. Program Description

Type of Material

- Instructional tool

Students

- Without disabilities
- Noncategorical

Ages

- Senior high school
- 18–21 years old

Other

- Not specified

Self-Determination Content

- Self-awareness: Identifying information about self—interests, strengths, weaknesses
- Goal setting: Deciding on desired outcomes
- Employment: Jobs, careers
- Education: Classes, sports, clubs, postsecondary education
- Housing and daily living: Home setting, daily living skills
- Personal: Recreation, leisure, legal, medical, health and wellness, relationships
- Community: Transportation, adult services, volunteering
- Communication

2. Materials Description

Materials Provided

- Replicable worksheets or masters
- Guide with background and overview
- Guide with directions for facilitating
- Visual semantic organizers

Materials Packaging and Presentation
- Spiral bound

Equipment Needed
- Flip chart
- VCR and monitor
- Camcorder
- Other (3-ring student notebooks)

Cost
- $30 (plus $4 for shipping)

3. Instructional Delivery

Setting
- Classroom and community based

Instructional Grouping
- Whole class (large and small groups)
- Partner and individual activities

Delivery Method
- Leader presents information
- Discovery/experiential: Participants complete activities related to objectives
- Group process: Participants interact with group members in activities related to objectives
- Community-based instruction: Experiences in the community

Leader
- Not specified

Number of Leaders
- One or two teachers

Leader Role
- Instructor: Leader directed
- Facilitator: Facilitates group interaction

Leader Training
- Not required

Lesson Sequence
- Set sequence for lessons within units
- Units may be taught selectively

Frequency of Lesson Use
- Several times per week or infused onto other material
- Flexible

Required Preparation
- Make copies
- Make visual aids (flip charts, overheads, etc.)
- Create examples
- Gather community information
- Order other curricular materials

Number of Lessons
- 47

Lesson Time
- 45 minutes

4. Instructional Components

Objectives
- Objectives stated

Prerequisite Skills
- Not identified

Quality of Instruction
- Targeted skills are clearly identified
- All activities align with objectives
- Examples used to teach concepts
- Cumulative review
- Spaced repetition
- Practice opportunities provided for targeted skills
- Modifications suggested for populations

Performance Evaluation Frequency
- Long-term mastery assessment

Performance Evaluation Type
- Self-report: Student indicates occurrence or magnitude of behavior
- Direct observation and recording: Observer uses measuring system to assess behavior as it occurs

Learner Activities
- Listening to information presented verbally (lecture)
- Reading and writing
- Group discussion
- Role play
- Community activities
- Question/answer
- Video taping of students and self-observation

- Homework
- Learning or self-management strategies
- Presentation

Generalization

- Rehearsal of behavior to approximate real situations
- Practice in more than one setting
- Practice rules for when to apply skills
- Conditional discriminations taught
- Frequent review of skills or incorporated into new skills
- Discussions of situations relevant to students in which they might use behavior

5. Research and Field Testing

Research

- None reported

Field Testing

- Field test reported, with outcome published elsewhere

ROCKETING INTO THE FUTURE: A STUDENT CONFERENCE LAUNCHING KIT

Robert Miller and Stephanie Corbey

Mankato State University, Interagency Office on Transition Services
657 Capital Square Building
550 Cedar
St. Paul, MN 55101
612-296-5660 Voice
612-297-2094 TDD/TTY

Abstract

Rocketing Into The Future is a do-it-yourself kit to assist in organizing and running local, regional, and state conferences to promote enrollment of students with disabilities in postsecondary education and training programs. Some of the resources in this kit include a sample budget, marketing materials, registration forms, agenda, pre-postassessment forms, letters to presenters, and participant confirmation. Possible users of this kit are transition interagency teams, postsecondary institutions, high school guidance counselors and educators, and others who wish to promote postsecondary education opportunities for youth with disabilities in their communities.

---

1. Program Description

Type of Material

- Teacher instruction or training

Students

- Not specified

Ages

- Middle/junior high school
- Senior high school

Other

- Educators
- Facilitators

Self-Determination Content

- Self-awareness: Identifying information about self—interests, strengths, weaknesses
- Personal self-advocacy: Acting on one's knowledge of oneself and one's rights
- Education: Classes, sports, clubs, postsecondary education

2. Materials Description

Materials Provided

- Replicable worksheets or masters

Materials Packaging and Presentation

- Loose pages
- Folder

Equipment Needed

- Not specified

Cost

- No information provided

3. Instructional Delivery

Setting

- Not specified

Instructional Grouping

- Not specified

Delivery Method

- Not specified

Leader

- Not specified

Number of Leaders

- Not specified

Leader Role

- Not specified

Leader Training

- Not specified

Lesson Sequence

- Not specified

Frequency of Lesson Use

- Not specified

Required Preparation

- Not specified

Number of Lessons

- Not specified

Lesson Time

- Not specified

4. Instructional Components

Objectives

- Not specified

Prerequisite Skills

- Not specified

Quality of Instruction

- Not specified

Performance Evaluation Frequency

- Not specified

Performance Evaluation Type

- Not specified

Learner Activities

- Not specified

Generalization

- Not specified

5. Research and Field Testing

Research

- Not specified

Field Testing

- Not specified

SELF-ADVOCACY: HOW STUDENTS WITH LEARNING DISABILITIES CAN MAKE THE TRANSITION FROM HIGH SCHOOL TO COLLEGE

Howard Eaton

Howard Eaton
3737 West 12th Avenue
Vancouver, BC
Canada V6R 2N7
604-222-1448

Abstract

This easy-to-read 60-page handbook is designed for use by high school students who have learning disabilities. In four sections, the author tells students about (1) the difficulties in going from high school to college, (2) the difficulties colleges have with students who have learning disabilities, (3) ways to improve your self-advocacy, and (4) checklists for transition. An accompanying audiotape presents the same information included in the handbook.

1. Program Description

Type of Material
- Instructional tool

Students
- With mild or moderate learning disabilities

Ages
- Senior high school

Other
- Not specified

Self-Determination Content
- Personal self-advocacy: Acting on one's knowledge of oneself and one's rights
- Education: Classes, sports, clubs, postsecondary education

2. Materials Description

Materials Provided
- Student text
- Audio material

Materials Packaging and Presentation
- Bound book
- Audiotape

Equipment Needed
- Tape recorder

Cost
- Less than $100

3. Instructional Delivery

Setting
- Not specified

Instructional Grouping
- Individual

Delivery Method
- Discovery/experiential: Participants complete activities related to objectives

Leader
- Not specified

Number of Leaders
- Not specified

Leader Role
- Not specified

Leader Training
- Not specified

Lesson Sequence
- Not specified

Frequency of Lesson Use
- Not specified

Required Preparation
- Not specified

Number of Lessons
- Not specified

Lesson Time
- Not specified

4. Instructional Components

Objectives
- Not specified

Prerequisite Skills
- Not specified

Quality of Instruction
- Not specified

Performance Evaluation Frequency
- Not specified

Performance Evaluation Type
- Not specified

Learner Activities
- Reading and writing
- Listening to audiotape

- *Generalization*
- Not specified

5. Research and Field Testing

Research
- None reported

Field Testing
- None reported
- Publisher testimonials: Publisher describes value of program

---

SELF-ADVOCACY FOR PEOPLE WITH DEVELOPMENTAL DISABILITIES

Cindy Rhoades and Philip Browning

James Stanfield Company
Drawer 125
P.O. Box 41058
Santa Barbara, CA 93140

Abstract

The purpose of this package is to promote and enhance the self-advocacy movement by teaching adults without disabilities to become advisors to self-advocacy groups. The lesson package includes a manual and a videotape (54 minutes). Together they address topics such as the self-advocacy philosophy, how to start new groups, and methods to conduct meetings. The five sections are (1) Speaking for Ourselves, (2) Starting a Self-Advocacy Group, (3) the Role of the Advisor in Self-Advocacy, (4) Officer Training, and (5) Organizing a Convention. Field testing showed that users of the materials were satisfied and that many of those trained started local self-advocacy groups.

1. Program Description

Type of Material
- Instructional tool

Students
- With mild or moderate learning disabilities or developmental disabilities

Ages
- 21 and older

Other
- Advisors of self-advocacy groups

Self-Determination Content
- Personal self-advocacy: Acting on one's knowledge of oneself and one's rights
- System self-advocacy: Taking action to change systems

2. Materials Description

Materials Provided
- Replicable worksheets or masters
- Awareness-building video
- Instructional video
- Overheads
- Guide with background and overview
- Guide with directions for facilitating

Materials Packaging and Presentation
- Envelope-package
- Spiral bound

Equipment Needed
- Overhead projector
- VCR and monitor

Cost
- Between $100 and $200

3. Instructional Delivery

Setting
- Community

Instructional Grouping
- Not specified

Delivery Method
- Leader presents information
- Discovery/experiential: Participants complete activities related to objectives
- Group process: Participants interact with group members in activities related to objectives

Leader
- Other—advisor

Number of Leaders
- Not specified

Leader Role
- Instructor: Leader directed
- Facilitator: Facilitates group interaction
- Coparticipant/colearner: Participates with group
- Model: Demonstrates process

Leader Training
- Not specified

Lesson Sequence
- Set sequence

Frequency of Lesson Use
- Flexible
- One-day workshop

Required Preparation
- Make visual aids (flip charts, overheads, etc.)
- Schedule guest speakers
- Schedule and/or train mentors
- Gather community information
- Other: Get VCR

Number of Lessons
- Five

Lesson Time
- 1 hour for use in a 1-day workshop

4. Instructional Components

Objectives
- Objectives stated

Prerequisite Skills

- Not identified

Quality of Instruction

- All activities align with objectives
- Modifications suggested for populations

Performance Evaluation Frequency

- Not specified

Performance Evaluation Type

- None

Learner Activities

- Listening to information presented verbally (lecture)

- Reading and writing
- Group discussion
- Role play
- Question/answer
- Videos

Generalization

- None

5. Research and Field Testing

Research

- User feedback: Users provide feedback on value of program

Field Testing

- None reported

SELF-ADVOCACY STRATEGY FOR EDUCATION AND TRANSITION PLANNING

Anthony K. Van Reusen, Candace S. Bos, Jean B. Schumaker, and Donald D. Deshler

Edge Enterprises, Inc.
P.O. Box 1304
Lawrence, KS 66044
913-749-1473

Abstract

This is a motivation strategy students use when preparing for and participating in an education conference, including the IEP and transition planning meetings. The strategy steps teach students how to get organized before a conference and how to communicate during the meeting. Students use the acronym "I PLAN" to remember the five strategy steps. Each letter cues the students to use a particular step. The five steps are (1) Inventory, (2) Provide your inventory information, (3) Listen and respond, (4) Ask questions, and (5) Name your goals. Several self-rated inventory checklists provide students the opportunity to evaluate their performance across several educational and community domains. This package is one of the motivation strategies of the Strategies Intervention Model from the University of Kansas.

1. Program Description

Type of Material
- Instructional tool

Students
- Noncategorical
- Mild and high risk

Ages
- Elementary school
- Middle school
- High school

Other
- Families

Self-Determination Content
- Self-awareness: Identifying information about self—interests, strengths, weaknesses
- Personal self-advocacy: Acting on one's knowledge of oneself and one's rights
- Person-centered planning: Student actively participating in planning activities such as planning one's own IEP
- Making choices and decisions
- Employment: Jobs, careers
- Education: Classes, sports, clubs, postsecondary education
- Housing and daily living: Home setting, daily living skills
- Personal: Recreation, leisure, legal, medical, health and wellness, relationships
- Community: Transportation, adult services, volunteering

2. Materials Description

Materials Provided
- Computer software
- Replicable worksheets or masters
- Guide with directions for facilitating

Materials Packaging and Presentation
- Book

Equipment Needed
- Overhead projector
- Other: Chalk board

Cost
- Less than $100

3. Instructional Delivery

Setting
- Not specified

Instructional Grouping
- Large group—greater than 10
- Small group—less than 10

Delivery Method
- Leader presents information

Leader
- Special educator
- General educator
- Support personnel

Number of Leaders
- Not specified

Leader Role
- Instructor: Leader directed

Leader Training
- Specific pretraining required

Lesson Sequence
- Set sequence

Frequency of Lesson Use
- Daily

Required Preparation
- Make copies
- Make visual aids (flip charts, overheads, etc.)
- Create examples
- Other: Make student folder
- List of upcoming courses

Number of Lessons
- Seven to eight

Lesson Time
- 6–7 hours
- 50-minute sessions
- Consecutive days

4. Instructional Components

Objectives

- Objectives stated
- Objectives measurable: Observable behavior, conditions, criteria

Prerequisite Skills

- Listed

Quality of Instruction

- Targeted skills are clearly identified
- Skill sequence
- All activities align with objectives
- Examples used to teach concepts
- Cumulative review
- Feedback procedures provided

Performance Evaluation Frequency

- Daily, weekly, or other regular assessment

Performance Evaluation Type

- Direct observation and recording: Observer uses measuring system to assess behavior as it occurs

Learner Activities

- Listening to information presented verbally (lecture)
- Reading and writing
- Group discussion
- Role play
- Learning or self-management strategies

Generalization

- Rehearsal of behavior to approximate real situations
- Practice rules for when to apply skills
- Frequent review of skills or incorporated into new skills
- Discussions of situations relevant to students in which they might use behavior

5. Research and Field Testing

Research

- Data included

Field Testing

- One group field test—pre- and post-performance without control group

---

SELF-DETERMINATION: A RESOURCE MANUAL FOR TEACHING AND LEARNING SELF-ADVOCACY

People First of Washington/Families Working Together
P.O. Box 648
Clarkston, WA 99403
509-758-1123

Abstract

This manual is designed to teach self-determination skills to students with developmental disabilities. The expected outcomes include increasing each person's sense of self-worth, responsible decision making, developing a clear future vision, and increasing awareness of each person's options and resources. A self-advocacy glossary and 11 topics are discussed in the manual. The topics include self-advocacy, self-esteem, individualism, friends, communication, decisions and options, respect, team building, the IEP process, assertiveness, and networking. Each chapter provides a definition, goals, topics, activities, and a list of resources.

1. Program Description

Type of Material
- Instructional tool

Students
- With mild or moderate learning disabilities

Ages
- Not specified

Other
- Families
- Educators
- Facilitators
- Friends
- Other professionals

Self-Determination Content
- Self-awareness: Identifying information about self—interests, strengths, weaknesses
- Personal self-advocacy: Acting on one's knowledge of oneself and one's rights
- Goal setting: Deciding on desired outcomes
- Person-centered planning: Student actively participating in planning activities such as planning one's own IEP
- Making choices and decisions
- Personal: Recreation, leisure, legal, medical, health and wellness, relationships

2. Materials Description

Materials Provided
- Replicable worksheets or masters
- Guide with directions for facilitating

Materials Packaging and Presentation
- Spiral bound

Equipment Needed
- Not specified

Cost
- Less than $100

3. Instructional Delivery

Setting
- Community
- After-school activity (e.g., extracurricular or evening activities)

Instructional Grouping
- Large group—greater than 10

Delivery Method
- Discovery/experiential: Participants complete activities related to objectives
- Group process: Participants interact with group members in activities related to objectives

Leader
- Not specified

Number of Leaders
- Not specified

Leader Role
- Not specified

Leader Training
- Not specified

Lesson Sequence
- Not specified

Frequency of Lesson Use
- Not specified

Required Preparation
- Make copies

Number of Lessons
- 11

Lesson Time
- Not specified

4. Instructional Components

Objectives
- Objectives stated
- Objectives measurable: Observable behavior, conditions, criteria

Prerequisite Skills
- Not specified

Quality of Instruction
- Targeted skills are clearly identified
- All activities align with objectives

Performance Evaluation Frequency
- Not applicable

Performance Evaluation Type
- None

Learner Activities
- Listening to information presented verbally (lecture)

- Question/answer
- Group discussion
- Role play

Generalization
- Not specified

5. Research and Field Testing

Research
- None reported

Field Testing
- None reported

SELF-DETERMINATION FOR YOUTH WITH DISABILITIES: A FAMILY EDUCATION CURRICULUM

Brian Abery

University of Minnesota
Institute on Community Integration
214 Pattee Hall, 150 Pillsbury Drive, S.E.
Minneapolis, MN 55455-0223
612-624-6328

Abstract

The purpose of this curriculum is to enable youth and young adults with disabilities to gain greater control of their lives by giving their families self-determination information and skills. This is not just for "other" family members since the individual with a disability is a full participant in all family activities. The curriculum consists of 15 modules that cover aspects of self-determination including such topics as "Creating a Personal Futures Plan," "Conducting Family Meetings," "Identifying Values and Goals," and "Realizing Your Vision." As the authors state, these "will be new concepts, requiring a good deal of reflection and discussion." The authors suggest that two facilitators lead the instruction. The lessons are presented to one family at a time. The facilitators need to secure additional material not included in the curriculum for several of the modules.

1. Program Description

Type of Material
- Instructional tool

Students
- Noncategorical

Ages
- Not specified

Other
- Families

Self-Determination Content
- Self-awareness: Identifying information about self—interests, strengths, weaknesses
- Personal self-advocacy: Acting on one's knowledge of oneself and one's rights
- System self-advocacy: Taking action to change systems
- Person-centered planning: Student actively participating in planning activities such as planning one's own IEP
- Goal setting: Deciding on desired outcomes
- Community: Transportation, adult services, volunteering
- Personal: Recreation, leisure, legal, medical, health and wellness, relationships

2. Materials Description

Materials Provided
- Replicable worksheets or masters
- Guide with background and overview
- Guide with directions for facilitating

Materials Packaging and Presentation
- Spiral bound

Equipment Needed
- VCR and monitor
- Flip chart
- Camcorder

Cost
- No information provided

3. Instructional Delivery

Setting
- Not specified, but assumed to take place in the homes of different family members

Instructional Grouping
- Not specified
- One family unit at a time

Delivery Method
- Leader presents information
- Discovery/experiential: Participants complete activities related to objectives
- Group process: Participants interact with group members in activities related to objectives

Leader
- Not specified

Number of Leaders
- Two

Leader Role
- Facilitator: Facilitates group interaction

Leader Training
- Not specified

Lesson Sequence
- Flexible sequence after a few required lessons are covered

Frequency of Lesson Use
- Flexible

Required Preparation
- Create examples
- Make copies
- Gather community information
- Order other curricular materials

Number of Lessons
- 15

Lesson Time
- 2 hours

4. Instructional Components

Objectives

- Objectives stated

Prerequisite Skills

- Not identified

Quality of Instruction

- Examples and nonexamples used to teach concepts
- All activities align with objectives

Performance Evaluation Frequency

- Not applicable

Performance Evaluation Type

- None

Learner Activities

- Listening to information presented verbally (lecture)
- Reading and writing
- Role play
- Question/answer
- Homework

Generalization

- Rehearsal of behavior to approximate real situations

5. Research and Field Testing

Research

- None reported

Field Testing

- None reported

SELF-DETERMINATION: PATHWAY TO INCLUSION Training Manual and Video

Pamela F. Miller and Sidney R. Miller

Department of Educational Psychology and Special Education
Southern Illinois University at Carbondale
Carbondale, IL 62901-4618
618-453-2311

Abstract

Self-Determination: Pathway to Inclusion is designed for individuals who work with high school students with emotional and behavioral disabilities. The three primary skill areas addressed in this program are self-determination skill development, assertiveness training, and self-management skills. This is an activity-based program in which students work together on a variety of problem-solving activities. The manual includes sections titled "Facilitative Listening Skills," "Assertiveness Component," "Communication Skills," and "Exercises for Self-Determination Mentors." A companion video, "Self-Determination: Pathway to Inclusion," shows the importance of self-determination in the lives of people with disabilities. In the video college students with disabilities describe what self-determination means to them.

1. Program Description

Type of Material
- Instructional tool

Students
- With mild or moderate learning disabilities or developmental disabilities

Ages
- Senior high school

Other
- Not specified

Self-Determination Content
- Making choices and decisions
- Personal self-advocacy: Acting on one's knowledge of oneself and one's rights

2. Materials Description

Materials Provided
- Guide with background and overview
- Guide with directions for facilitating
- Replicable worksheets or masters
- Awareness-building video

Materials Packaging and Presentation
- Spiral bound

Equipment Needed
- Overhead projector
- Flip chart
- VCR and monitor

Cost
- No information provided

3. Instructional Delivery

Setting
- Not specified

Instructional Grouping
- Small group—less than 10

Delivery Method
- Discovery/experiential: Participants complete activities related to objectives
- Group process: Participants interact with group members in activities related to objectives

Leader
- Not specified

Number of Leaders
- One

Leader Role
- Facilitator: Facilitates group interaction

Leader Training
- Not specified

Lesson Sequence
- Not specified

Frequency of Lesson Use
- Not specified

Required Preparation
- Make copies
- Make visual aids (flip charts, overheads, etc.)
- Create examples
- Schedule and/or train mentors

Number of Lessons
- Difficult to determine

Lesson Time
- Not specified

4. Instructional Components

Objectives
- Objectives stated

Prerequisite Skills
- Not specified

Quality of Instruction
- Examples used to teach concepts
- Practice opportunities provided for targeted skills

Performance Evaluation Frequency
- Not specified

Performance Evaluation Type

- Direct observation and recording: Observer uses measuring system to assess behavior as it occurs

Learner Activities

- Group discussion
- Role play
- Games
- Learning or self-management strategies
- Listening to information presented verbally (lecture)
- Question/answer
- Mentoring

Generalization

- Rehearsal of behavior to approximate real situations

5. Research and Field Testing

Research

- None reported

Field Testing

- None reported

SELF-DETERMINATION PROFILE, IT'S MY LIFE-PREFERENCE: PREFERENCE BASED PLANNING, MY LIFE PLANNER, PROFILE DECKS, AND DIGNITY BASED MODELS

Emilee Curtis

New Hats Inc.
P.O. Box 57567
Salt Lake City, UT 84157
801-268-9811

Abstract

The New Hats organization distributes several different instructional packages. A facilitator uses these materials to show how students or adults with disabilities can take an active role in making decisions, self-advocating, and creating their own lifestyle plans and goals. The *Self-Determination Profile* uses illustrated cards to help the person discover preferences and interests across five accomplishment areas (community presence, community participation, choice, competence, and respect). It's My Life-Preference provides a booklet of activities that help individuals set goals and plan their own goal setting meetings. My Life Planner contains a set of planners to help individuals plan their lives across five areas. Several profile decks accompany the lessons to help individuals process their decisions and choices. These include The Self-Determination Profile, The Profile Deck, The Hat Card Deck, and The I Want My Dream Deck. The workbook on the Dignity Based Model contains a toolbox of ideas for those who work with individuals with disabilities to help them realize their dreams in a respectful manner and with dignity.

1. Program Description

Type of Material
- Instructional tool
- Assessment tool

Students
- Without disabilities
- Noncategorical

Ages
- Not specified

Other
- Educators
- Facilitators

Self-Determination Content
- Self-awareness: Identifying information about self—interests, strengths, weaknesses
- Personal self-advocacy: Acting on one's knowledge of oneself and one's rights
- Goal setting: Deciding on desired outcomes
- Self-evaluation: Comparing one's performance to a standard
- Person-centered planning: Student actively participating in planning activities such as planning one's own IEP
- Making choices and decisions
- Employment: Jobs, careers
- Housing and daily living: Home setting, daily living skills
- Personal: Recreation, leisure, legal, medical, health and wellness, relationships
- Community: Transportation, adult services, volunteering

2. Materials Description

Materials Provided
- Replicable worksheets or masters
- Activity cards
- Guide with directions for facilitating

Materials Packaging and Presentation
- Three-ring binder
- Box
- Spiral bound

Equipment Needed
- Not specified

Cost
- Less than $100 for each component

3. Instructional Delivery

Setting
- Not specified

Instructional Grouping
- Not specified

Delivery Method
- Leader presents information
- Discovery/experiential: Participants complete activities related to objectives
- Group process: Participants interact with group members in activities related to objectives

Leader
- Not specified

Number of Leaders
- Not specified

Leader Role
- Facilitator: Facilitates group interaction

Leader Training
- Specific pretraining required

Lesson Sequence
- Not specified

Frequency of Lesson Use
- Not specified

Required Preparation
- Gather community information
- Make copies

Number of Lessons
- Not specified

Lesson Time
- Not specified

4. Instructional Components

Objectives

- Objectives stated

Prerequisite Skills

- Listed

Quality of Instruction

- All activities align with objectives
- Cumulative review
- Practice opportunities provided for targeted skills
- Feedback procedures provided
- Targeted skills are clearly identified

Performance Evaluation Frequency

- Not specified

Performance Evaluation Type

- Self-report: Student indicates occurrence or magnitude of behavior

Learner Activities

- Listening to information presented verbally (lecture)
- Reading and writing
- Group discussion
- Community activities
- Games
- Mentoring
- Learning or self-management strategies

Generalization

- Rehearsal of behavior to approximate real situations

5. Research and Field Testing

Research

- User feedback: Users provide feedback on value of program

Field Testing

- None reported

SELF-DETERMINATION: THE ROAD TO PERSONAL FREEDOM

Leslie Martin and Dale Carter

Self-Determination Team
Protection and Advocacy System
1720 Louisiana N.E., Suite 204
Albuquerque, NM 87110
505-256-3100

Abstract

This curriculum presents several concepts and teacher strategies and provides opportunities to practice what it takes to be self-determined. The curriculum is a guide to daily classroom and community living, not a set of lessons that are to be done in a class at a certain time each week. The authors are firm in their belief that the concepts need to be infused into all curriculum content areas. Because of this, no lessons are presented; rather, conceptual units are provided. Most units follow the same structure: a proverb, a self-determination example, vocabulary, unit concept, and the unit goal. Unit titles include "Introduction to Self-Determination," "Expanding Roles: Practice Makes Perfect," "Facing Facts: Disabilities and Accommodations," "The Big R's: Rights and Responsibilities," and "Celebration of Self." Many examples from New Mexico are included, such as New Mexico resources, self-determined New Mexicans, New Mexico music, and books written by New Mexicans. *Self-determination* refers to the skills and attitudes that encourage individuals and groups to set and then reach their goals.

1. Program Description

Type of Material

- Instructional tool

Students

- Noncategorical

Ages

- Senior high school

Other

- Not specified

Self-Determination Content

- Self-awareness: Identifying information about self—interests, strengths, weaknesses
- Goal setting: Deciding on desired outcomes
- Community: Transportation, adult services, volunteering
- Person-centered planning: Student actively participating in planning activities such as planning one's own IEP
- Personal: Recreation, leisure, legal, medical, health and wellness, relationships

2. Materials Description

Materials Provided

- Replicable worksheets or masters
- Guide with background and overview
- Guide with directions for facilitating

Materials Packaging and Presentation

- Three-ring binder

Equipment Needed

- VCR and monitor

Cost

- Less than $100

3. Instructional Delivery

Setting

- Not specified
- General education class (mentioned that could be used here)

Instructional Grouping

- Not specified

Delivery Method

- Leader presents information
- Discovery/experiential: Participants complete activities related to objectives
- Group process: Participants interact with group members in activities related to objectives

Leader

- Not specified ("Teacher")

Number of Leaders

- Not specified

Leader Role

- Instructor: Leader directed

Leader Training

- Not specified

Lesson Sequence

- Flexible sequence

Frequency of Lesson Use

- Flexible

Required Preparation

- Make copies
- Secure community sites
- Schedule guest speakers
- Gather community information

Number of Lessons

- Not specified

Lesson Time

- Not specified (not set up in lessons)

4. Instructional Components

Objectives

- Objectives stated

Prerequisite Skills

- Not identified

Quality of Instruction

- Targeted skills are clearly identified

- All activities align with objectives
- Modifications suggested for populations

Performance Evaluation Frequency

- Daily, weekly, or other regular assessment

Performance Evaluation Type

- Other options: Short-answer and paper/pencil tests

Learner Activities

- Listening to information presented verbally (lecture)
- Reading and writing
- Group discussion
- Role play

- Games
- Community activities
- Question/answer
- Videos

Generalization

- Other: Paper/pencil test/last page of each section

5. Research and Field Testing

Research

- None reported

Field Testing

- Field test reported, but no data available

SELF-DETERMINATION TRAINING: JOURNEY TO INDEPENDENCE

Michael Wehmeyer and Hank Bersani, Jr.
Iowa Department of Education
510 East 12th Street
Des Moines, IA 50319
515-281-4114

Abstract

This manual provides instructional materials to empower students with disabilities and their family members to play active roles in the transition planning process. The purpose is not to lead students to mastery levels, but rather to increase awareness that students and family members should take an active role in planning for the future. The materials introduce students and their family members to self-determination and self-advocacy through identifying student interests, abilities, and expectations. The materials are designed to be used in a workshop format. Four modules are used: (1) *Are You Ready to Travel*; (2) *Be Part of the Team*; (3) *Know the Territory*; and (4) *You're On the Way*. Facilitator materials are provided, including overheads and evaluation checklists.

1. Program Description

Type of Material

- Instructional tool for parent and student instruction

Students

- With mild or moderate learning disabilities or developmental disabilities
- With mild or moderate behavioral or emotional disabilities

Ages

- Middle school
- Senior high school (for students beginning the transition process)

Other

- Family members (as possible facilitators or as workshop participants)

Self-Determination Content

- Self-awareness: Identifying information about self—interests, strengths, weaknesses
- Personal self-advocacy: Acting on one's knowledge of oneself and one's rights
- Making choices and decisions

2. Materials Description

Materials Provided

- Replicable worksheets or masters
- Overheads
- Guide with background and overview
- Guide with directions for facilitating

Materials Packaging and Presentation

- Three-ring binder

Equipment Needed

- Overhead projector
- Flip chart
- VCR and monitor
- Work table
- Name tags
- Miscellaneous items

Cost

- No information provided

3. Instructional Delivery

Setting

- Not specified

Instructional Grouping

- Not specified

Delivery Method

- Leader presents information
- Discovery/experiential: Participants complete activities related to objectives
- Group process: Participants interact with group members in activities related to objectives

Leader

- Special educator
- Individual with disability
- Parent

Number of Leaders

- Three

Leader Role

- Instructor: To present information
- Facilitator: Facilitates group interaction

Leader Training

- Not specified

Lesson Sequence

- Set sequence

Frequency of Lesson Use

- Not specified

Required Preparation

- Schedule guest speakers
- Create examples
- Make copies
- Gather community information
- Order other curricular materials

Number of Lessons

- Four modules

Lesson Time

- Each module is 2 hours long

4. Instructional Components

Objectives

- Objectives stated

Prerequisite Skills

- None listed except that program is for students with mild disabilities

Quality of Instruction

- Targeted skills are clearly identified
- Cumulative review

Performance Evaluation Frequency

- Not applicable

Performance Evaluation Type

- None

Learner Activities

- Listening to information presented verbally (lecture)
- Group discussion
- Question/answer
- Mentoring
- Reading and writing

Generalization

- Discussions of situations relevant to students in which they might use behavior

5. Research and Field Testing

Research

- None reported

Field Testing

- None reported

STEPS TO SELF-DETERMINATION Instructor's Guide and Student Activity Book

Sharon Field and Alan Hoffman

and

SELF-DETERMINATION KNOWLEDGE SCALE

Alan Hoffman, Sharon Field, and Shlomo Sawilowsky

Pro-Ed Publishing Company
8700 Shoal Creek Boulevard
Austin, TX 78757-6897
800-397-7633

Also available from:

The Council for Exceptional Children
1920 Association Drive
Reston, VA 20191-1589
888-232-7323

Abstract

This curriculum and assessment tool supports students in developing skills, knowledge, and experiences to help them be more self-determined. The activities engage students in experiences designed to increase their self-awareness and self-esteem and provides instruction in skills to assist them in reaching their goals. The curriculum follows a five-step model: (1) Know yourself, (2) value yourself, (3) plan, (4) act, and (5) experience outcomes and learn. Each curriculum activity relates back to one of these steps. The lessons begin with a 6-hour workshop session, followed by 16 weekly sessions that take place in a scheduled class or as an extracurricular activity. The 6-hour workshop can be taught as six separate 1-hour sessions. The 16 sessions include topics such as "What is Important to Me?" "Setting Long-Term Goals," "Creative Barrier Breaking," "Assertive Communication," "Negotiation," and "Conflict Resolution." Teachers are encouraged to participate in the activities as colearners with the students. Included is a student activity book that provides copies of all student worksheets. The "Self-Determination Knowledge Scale" provides a pretest and posttest method of measuring student progress.

1. Program Description

Type of Material

- Instructional tool
- Assessment tool

Students

- Without disabilities
- Noncategorical

Ages

- Middle/junior high school
- Senior high school
- 18–21 years old

Other

- Families
- Friends

Self-Determination Content

- Self-awareness: Identifying information about self—interests, strengths, weaknesses
- Personal self-advocacy: Acting on one's knowledge of oneself and one's rights
- Goal setting: Deciding on desired outcomes
- Self-evaluation: Comparing one's performance to a standard
- Adjustment: Making adaptations to achieve desired outcomes
- Employment: Jobs, careers
- Housing and daily living: Home setting, daily living skills
- Personal: Recreation, leisure, legal, medical, health and wellness, relationships
- Community: Transportation, adult services, volunteering
- Conflict resolution and negotiations

2. Materials Description

Materials Provided

- Replicable worksheets or masters
- Consumable written materials
- Overheads
- Guide with background and overview
- Guide with directions for facilitating
- Other: A pre-post assessment tool

Materials Packaging and Presentation

- Bound

Equipment Needed

- Overhead projector
- Flip chart

Cost

- Less than $100

3. Instructional Delivery

Setting

- General education class
- Special education class
- Resource room
- After-school activity

Instructional Grouping

- Small group—less than 10
- Large group—greater than 10

Delivery Method

- Leader presents information
- Discovery/experiential: Participants complete activities related to objectives
- Group process: Participants interact with group members in activities related to objectives

Leader

- Special educator
- General educator
- Support personnel

Number of Leaders

- One–three

Leader Role

- Facilitator: Facilitates group interaction
- Coparticipant/colearner: Participates with group
- Model: Demonstrate process

Leader Training

- None required
- Inservice training available on request

Lesson Sequence

- Set sequence

Frequency of Lesson Use

- Not specified

Required Preparation

- Make copies
- Make visual aids (flip charts, overheads, etc.)
- Create examples and role plays
- Schedule guest speakers
- Gather community information

Number of Lessons

- 18

Lesson Time

- Average 55 minutes
- First workshop is 6 hours long, or can be taught as six 55-minute sessions

4. Instructional Components

Objectives

- Objectives stated

Prerequisite Skills

- None identified

Quality of Instruction

- Targeted skills are clearly identified
- Skill sequence
- All activities align with objectives
- Examples and nonexamples used to teach concepts
- Cumulative review
- Spaced repetition
- Practice opportunities provided for targeted skills
- Feedback procedures provided
- Modifications suggested for populations

Performance Evaluation Frequency

- Not specified

Performance Evaluation Type

- Pretest and/or posttest
- Rating scales checklists: Others indicate occurrence or magnitude of behavior
- Self-report: Student indicates occurrence or magnitude of behavior

Learner Activities

- Listening to information presented verbally (lecture)
- Reading and writing
- Group discussion
- Role play
- Question/answer
- Homework
- Learning or self-management strategies

Generalization

- Frequent review of skills or incorporated into new skills
- Discussions of situations relevant to students in which they might use behavior

5. Research and Field Testing

Research

- Controlled study

Field Testing

- Field-test results reported elsewhere found significant difference pre to post on knowledge and behavior associated with self-determination

A STUDENT'S GUIDE TO THE IEP and HELPING STUDENTS DEVELOP THEIR IEPS + AUDIOTAPE

NICHCY: The National Information Center for Children and Youth with Disabilities

National Information Center for Children and Youth with Disabilities
P.O. Box 1492
Washington, DC 20013-1492
1-800-695-0285

Abstract

This package is written for students, parents, and teachers who would like to help students with disabilities become involved in developing their own individualized education programs (IEPs). It is accompanied by an audiotape of teachers, parents, and students discussing how they have helped students become active participants in the IEP process. NICHY hopes that, together, the guide and the tape will answer many questions about involving students in planning their own education. The materials help all parties involved realize that students can learn (a) more about their strengths and skills and be able to tell others; (b) more about their disability, including how to talk about and explain the nature of their disability to others; (c) what accommodations are and what types of accommodations might help them succeed in the classroom; (d) how to speak for themselves; (e) skills necessary for self-determination and independent decision-making; (f) about the goals and objectives that form the basis for their education and why these goals and objectives are important for them; and, ultimately, (g) to become more involved in their own education.

1. Program Description

Type of Material

- Instructional tool

Students

- Not specified

Ages

- Middle/junior high school
- Senior high school

Other

- Families
- Educators
- Facilitators
- Other professionals

Self-Determination Content

- Self-awareness: Identifying information about self—interests, strengths, weaknesses
- Personal self-advocacy: Acting on one's knowledge of oneself and one's rights
- Goal setting: Deciding on desired outcomes
- Self-evaluation: Comparing one's performance to a standard
- Person-centered planning: Student actively participating in planning activities such as planning one's own IEP
- Making choices and decisions
- Education: Classes, sports, clubs, postsecondary education

2. Materials Description

Materials Provided

- Replicable worksheets or masters
- Audio materials
- Guide with background and overview
- Guide with directions for facilitating

Materials Packaging and Presentation
- Pamphlets

Equipment Needed
- Tape recorder
- Book and tape

Cost
- Free as long as supplies last

3. Instructional Delivery

Setting
- Not specified

Instructional Grouping
- Not specified

Delivery Method
- Leader presents information
- Discovery/experiential: Participants complete activities related to objectives
- Group process: Participants interact with group members in activities related to objectives

Leader
- Not specified

Number of Leaders
- Not specified

Leader Role
- Instructor: Leader directed
- Facilitator: Facilitates group interaction
- Model: Demonstrates process

Leader Training
- Not specified

Lesson Sequence
- Set sequence

Frequency of Lesson Use
- Flexible

Required Preparation
- Make copies
- Make visual aids (flip charts, overheads, etc.)
- Create examples

- Order other curricular materials

Number of Lessons
- Not specified

Lesson Time
- Flexible

4. Instructional Components

Objectives
- Not specified

Prerequisite Skills
- None identified

Quality of Instruction
- Targeted skills are clearly identified
- Examples used to teach concepts

Performance Evaluation Frequency
- None

Performance Evaluation Type
- None

Learner Activities
- Listening to information presented verbally (lecture)
- Reading and writing
- Group discussion
- Role play
- Question/answer
- Homework
- Listening to audiotape

Generalization
- Rehearsal of behavior to approximate real situations
- Discussions of situations relevant to students in which they might use behavior

5. Research and Field Testing

Research
- User feedback: Users provide feedback on value of program

Field Testing
- Field test reported, but no outcome data presented

TAKE CHARGE and TAKE CHARGE FOR THE FUTURE

Laurie Powers
Oregon Health Sciences University
Child Development and Rehabilitation Center
P.O. Box 574
Portland, OR 97207-0574

Abstract

Take Charge is designed to facilitate self-determination and competence by reducing learned helplessness and increasing mastery motivation and self-efficacy. This is done through four major components: (1) learning self-determination skills; (2) mentorship; (3) peer support; and (4) parent support. Achievement, partnership, and coping are the three generic strategies used in *Take Charge*. Through these lessons middle school students and freshmen learn what their dreams are and how to set goals, problem solve, negotiate, manage frustration, and track their progress. *Take Charge for the Future* specifically addresses transition planning and is intended for sophomores and juniors. In this second lesson package emphasis is placed upon students' learning the skills needed to participate actively in their own transition planning and implementation process. Five major steps comprise the *Take Charge for the Future* lessons: (1) dream; (2) set goals; (3) get it together; (4) take care of business; and (5) keep it going. Included are several companion guides that cover work, friendship, and college. A guide for parents is also included.

1. Program Description

Type of Material

- Instructional tool

Students

- Noncategorical

Ages

- Middle school students and freshmen (*Take Charge*)
- Sophomores and juniors (*Take Charge for the Future*)

Other

- Families

Self-Determination Content

- Self-awareness: Identifying information about self—interests, strengths, weaknesses
- Personal self-advocacy: Acting on one's knowledge of oneself and one's rights
- Goal setting: Deciding on desired outcomes
- Adjustment: Making adaptations to achieve desired outcomes
- Person-centered planning: Student actively participating in planning activities such as planning one's own IEP
- Making choices and decisions
- Employment: Jobs, careers
- Education: Classes, sports, clubs, postsecondary education
- Housing and daily living: Home setting, daily living skills
- Personal: Recreation, leisure, legal, medical, health and wellness, relationships
- Self-evaluation: Comparing one's performance to a standard
- Community: Transportation, adult services, volunteering

2. Materials Description

Materials Provided

- Replicable worksheets or masters
- Guide with background and overview (for parents)

Materials Packaging and Presentation

- Three-ring binder

Equipment Needed

- Not specified

Cost

- No information provided

3. Instructional Delivery

Setting

- Not specified

Instructional Grouping

- Not specified

Delivery Method

- Discovery/experiential: Participants complete activities related to objectives
- Group process: Participants interact with group members in activities related to objectives

Leader

- Not specified

Number of Leaders

- Not specified

Leader Role

- Facilitator: Facilitates group interaction

Leader Training

- Not specified

Lesson Sequence

- Not specified

Frequency of Lesson Use

- Flexible

Required Preparation

- Make copies

Number of Lessons

- 30 for *Take Charge*
- Variable for *Take Charge for the Future*

Lesson Time

- 1 hour is average lesson time

4. Instructional Components

Objectives

- Not specified

Prerequisite Skills

- None identified

Quality of Instruction

- Skill sequence
- Targeted skills are clearly identified
- Spaced repetition
- Practice opportunities provided for targeted skills
- Feedback procedures provided
- Examples used to teach concepts

Performance Evaluation Frequency

- Not specified

Performance Evaluation Type

- Self-report: Student indicates occurrence or magnitude of behavior

Learner Activities

- Reading and writing
- Question/answer
- Homework
- Group discussion
- Role play
- Mentoring
- Learning or self-management strategies

Generalization

- Rehearsal of behavior to approximate real situations
- Discussions of situations relevant to students in which they might use behavior
- Practice rules for when to apply skills

5. Research and Field Testing

Research

- None reported

Field Testing

- None reported

THE TRANS-PLAN: PLANNING FOR YOUR FUTURE

Wynne Begun, Linda Minor, Bev Silvers, and Pat Witcher
Johnson County School Districts
Blue Valley North High School
12200 Lamar
Overland Park, KS 66209
913-345-7318

Abstract

The Trans-Plan is a teacher-developed lesson package designed for developing self-advocacy and transition planning strategies. It is based on the *Self-Advocacy Strategy* from Edge Enterprises (also described in this chapter). It consists of eight units: (1) transition and future strategy planning; (2) federal and state legislation; (3) transition resources; (4) communication skills; (5) self-awareness; (6) self-advocacy; (7) goal setting; and (8) IEP implementation. Each unit contains a section on background materials that provides educators with needed facts behind the unit concepts and a collection of curriculum materials. The authors brought together the best of many resources to help explain and teach crucial transition and self-determination concepts. It ends with students using the *Self-Advocacy Strategy* to actively participate in their own IEP meetings

1. Program Description

Type of Material
- Instructional tool

Students
- Noncategorical

Ages
- Middle or junior high school
- Senior high school
- 18–21 years old

Other
- Not specified

Self-Determination Content
- Self-awareness: Identifying information about self—interests, strengths, weaknesses
- Personal self-advocacy: Acting on one's knowledge of oneself and one's rights
- System self-advocacy: Taking action to change systems
- Goal setting: Deciding on desired outcomes
- Self-evaluation: Comparing one's performance to a standard
- Person-centered planning: Student actively participating in planning activities such as planning one's own IEP

2. Materials Description

Materials Provided
- Replicable worksheets or masters
- Awareness-building video
- Instructional video
- Guide with background and overview
- Copies of many articles and curriculum forms

Materials Packaging and Presentation
- Loose pages

Equipment Needed
- VCR and monitor

Cost
- No information provided

3. Instructional Delivery

Setting

- Not specified

Instructional Grouping

- Small group—less than 10
- Individual (one-to-one tutoring)

Delivery Method

- Leader presents information
- Discovery/experiential: Participants complete activities related to objectives
- Group process: Participants interact with group members in activities related to objectives

Leader

- Special educator
- Support personnel
- Individual with disability

Number of Leaders

- Not specified

Leader Role

- Instructor: Leader directed
- Facilitator: Facilitates group interaction

Leader Training

- Not specified

Lesson Sequence

- Not specified

Frequency of Lesson Use

- Not specified

Required Preparation

- Make copies
- Create examples
- Schedule guest speakers
- Order other curricular materials

Number of Lessons

- Not specified

Lesson Time

- Not specified

4. Instructional Components

Objectives

- Objectives stated

Prerequisite Skills

- None identified

Quality of Instruction

- Targeted skills are clearly identified
- All activities align with objectives
- Practice opportunities provided for targeted skills

Performance Evaluation Frequency

- No set schedule to use the student checklist

Performance Evaluation Type

- Other: Checklist for students
- Resource information

Learner Activities

- Listening to information presented verbally (lecture)
- Reading and writing
- Group discussion
- Role play
- Question/answer
- Videos
- Homework
- Learning or self-management strategies

Generalization

- Not specified

5. Research and Field Testing

Research

- None reported

Field Testing

- Field test reported, but no outcome data presented

TRANSITION ISSUES CURRICULUM: A CURRICULUM FOR STUDENTS IN SPECIAL EDUCATION WITH MODERATE NEEDS TO PLAN AND PREPARE FOR THEIR OWN TRANSITION

Lisa Carter

Colorado Department of Education/Special Education Services
201 East Colfax, Room 300
Denver, CO 80203
303-866-6694

Abstract

This curriculum is designed to help students answer crucial questions, including the following: What are your greatest dreams? What are your greatest fears? What barriers might get in the way of your accomplishing your goals? What resources will overcome these barriers? How can school resources help you reach your goals? Is there anything the school or agencies are doing for you now that you could do for yourself? What compensation strategies do you need to develop successful independent living skills? Key to many activities is the Transition Game, which is a tool for students to conceptualize the transition planning process. In playing the game a student sets a goal, then plays the game on a football-like board. Several topic areas are discussed, including educational issues, career and employment issues, community and residential issues, recreation and leisure issues, legal and medical issues, and social and interpersonal issues. Detailed activities facilitate understanding of each topical area.

1. Program Description

Type of Material

- Instructional tool

Students

- With mild or moderate learning disabilities or developmental disabilities
- With mild or moderate behavioral or emotional disabilities

Ages

- Middle/junior high school
- Senior high school

Other

- Not specified

Self-Determination Content

- Self-awareness: Identifying information about self—interests, strengths, weaknesses
- Person-centered planning: Student actively participating in planning activities such as planning one's own IEP
- Goal setting: Deciding on desired outcomes
- Making choices and decisions
- Employment: Jobs, careers
- Education: Classes, sports, clubs, postsecondary education
- Housing and daily living: Home setting, daily living skills
- Personal: Recreation, leisure, legal, medical, health and wellness, relationships
- Community: Transportation, adult services, volunteering
- Self-evaluation: Comparing one's performance to a standard

2. Materials Description

Materials Provided

- Replicable worksheets or masters
- Games (made by teacher or purchased from Colorado Department of Education)
- Guide with background and overview
- Guide with directions for facilitating

Materials Packaging and Presentation

- Spiral bound

Equipment Needed

- Overhead projector

Cost

- Less than $100

3. Instructional Delivery

Setting

- Resource room (designed for students served in this setting)
- Community

Instructional Grouping

- Not specified

Delivery Method

- Leader presents information
- Discovery/experiential: Participants complete activities related to objectives
- Group process: Participants interact with group members in activities related to objectives
- Community-based instruction: Experiences in the community

Leader

- Not specified

Number of Leaders

- Not specified

Leader Role

- Instructor: Leader directed
- Facilitator: Facilitates group interaction
- Model: Demonstrates process

Leader Training

- Not specified

Lesson Sequence

- Not specified

Frequency of Lesson Use

- Not specified

Required Preparation

- Make copies
- Make visual aids (flip charts, overheads, etc.)
- Create examples
- Secure community sites
- Schedule guest speakers

Number of Lessons

- Seven units: Each section contains many objectives and activities

Lesson Time

- Not specified

4. Instructional Components

Objectives

- Objectives stated

Prerequisite Skills

- None identified

Quality of Instruction

- Targeted skills are clearly identified
- Examples and nonexamples used to teach concepts
- All activities align with objectives
- Spaced repetition
- Practice opportunities provided for targeted skills

Performance Evaluation Frequency

- Not specified

Performance Evaluation Type

- Rating scales checklists: Others indicate occurrence or magnitude of behavior
- Self-report: Student indicates occurrence or magnitude of behavior

Learner Activities

- Listening to information presented verbally (lecture)
- Reading and writing
- Group discussion
- Role play
- Games (must be purchased from Colorado Department of Education or made by teacher)
- Community activities
- Question/answer
- Volunteering
- Jobs

Generalization

- Rehearsal of behavior to approximate real situations
- Practice in more than one setting
- Frequent review of skills or incorporated into new skills
- Discussions of situations relevant to students in which they might use behavior

5. Research and Field Testing

Research

- None reported

Field Testing

- None reported

WHOSE FUTURE IS IT ANYWAY? A STUDENT-DIRECTED TRANSITION PLANNING PROCESS

Michael Wehmeyer and Kathy Kelchner (Coach's Guide by Michael Wehmeyer, Kathy Kelchner, and Margaret Lawrence)

The Arc National Headquarters
500 East Border Street, Suite 300
Arlington, TX 76010
800-433-5255

Abstract

This instructional package provides students the opportunity to acquire the knowledge and confidence to take part in the transition process as equal partners. The package emphasizes disability as a part of the human condition and stresses that students need to be aware of their own learning abilities and needs. Each session teaches students something they can use in their transition or other educational meeting. Students learn (a) how to write and track goals, (b) how to identify community resources, (c) how informed consent affects them, (d) how to communicate in small groups, and (e) how to participate in a meeting. Students select a coach to help them through the process. The six major parts of the program are (1) getting to know you; (2) making decisions; (3) how to get what you need; (4) goals, objectives, and the future; (5) communication; and (6) thank you. Students use the materials on their own: They read and complete the 40 lessons for 1 to 2 hours each week. The materials are designed for students to read and complete independently. The coach is available to assist and facilitate completing the readings and activities. The desired outcome is that students learn the skills they need to play a meaningful role in their transition planning process. A *Coach's Guide* is included. It describes the teacher's role and how to use the materials and provides tips to help students successfully accomplish each lesson.

1. Program Description

Type of Material

- Instructional tool

Students

- With mild or moderate cognitive and developmental disabilities
- With mild or moderate learning disabilities or developmental disabilities

Ages

- Senior high school, ages 14 through 21
- Middle/junior high school

Other

- Not specified

Self-Determination Content

- Person-centered planning: Student actively participating in planning activities such as planning one's own IEP
- Personal self-advocacy: Acting on one's knowledge of oneself and one's rights
- System self-advocacy: Taking action to change systems
- Self-efficacy: Belief that one can accomplish one's goals
- Employment: Jobs, careers
- Self-evaluation: Comparing one's performance to a standard
- Education: Classes, sports, clubs, postsecondary education
- Housing and daily living: Home setting, daily living skills
- Self-awareness: Identifying information about self—interests, strengths, weaknesses
- Making choices and decisions
- Goal setting: Deciding on desired outcomes
- Personal: Recreation, leisure, legal, medical, health and wellness, relationships
- Community: Transportation, adult services, volunteering

2. Materials Description

Materials Provided

- Guide with background and overview
- Guide with directions for facilitating
- Consumable written materials

Materials Packaging and Presentation

- Soft-sided book

Equipment Needed

- Not specified

Cost

- Contact author

3. Instructional Delivery

Setting

- Not specified: Students do on their own; thus could be completed in many places

Instructional Grouping

- Individualized use, but can be used in a group

Delivery Method

- Discovery/experiential: Participants complete activities related to objectives
- Group process: Participants interact with group members in activities related to objectives
- Leader presents information

Leader

- Special educator

Number of Leaders

- One

Leader Role

- Facilitator: Facilitates group interaction (done as a coach)
- Instructor: Leader directed; leader presents information

Leader Training

- Not specified

Lesson Sequence

- Set sequence

Frequency of Lesson Use

- Weekly

Required Preparation

- Make copies
- Create examples
- Make worksheets
- Gather community information

Number of Lessons

- 36

Lesson Time

- 1–2 hours a week over a school year

4. Instructional Components

Objectives

- Objectives stated
- Objectives not measurable—observable behavior, conditions, criteria

Prerequisite Skills

- None identified

Quality of Instruction

- Targeted skills are clearly identified
- Skill sequence
- All activities align with objectives
- Cumulative review
- Spaced repetition
- Practice opportunities provided for targeted skills
- Examples used to teach concepts

Performance Evaluation Frequency

- Not specified

Performance Evaluation Type

- Not specified

Learner Activities

- Reading and writing
- Group discussion
- Learning or self-management strategies

Generalization

- Discussions of situations relevant to students in which they might use behavior
- Frequent review of skills or incorporated into new skills

5. Research and Field Testing

Research

- Study published elsewhere shows major change in students' self-determination

Field Testing

- Field test reported, but no outcome data presented

Special

- Written in a very funny style that many students will enjoy

Key Issues and Future Directions in Self-Determination

The purpose of this chapter is to

- Examine and discuss current issues related to self-determination.
- Identify research and development needs in the area of self-determination.

How Can Self-Determination Produce Better Results in Employment and Community Living for Persons with Disabilities?

Self-determination skills focusing on such characteristics as decision making, goal setting, self-actualization, and an internal locus of control should provide students with some future-oriented vision. As indicated by Ward (1988) and discussed in Chapter 1, acquisition of the personal characteristics that lead to self-determination is a developmental process that begins in early childhood and continues throughout the adult years. Therefore, no one, including students without disabilities, will automatically become self-determined at some given age—whether it is 18, 21, age of majority, or age of maturity—without some educational focus on the skills related to self-determination. If a primary goal of special education is to ensure better results in employment and community living, as suggested by Hehir (1994), it is critical that skills related to self-determination be taught to students with disabilities as early as possible. Instruction in these skills should take on an increasingly more complex focus as students become older.

How can we measure better results in employment and community living for persons with disabilities? A key must be consumer satisfaction—that is, that persons with disabilities are more satisfied with where they live and work. If consumers are satisfied, it is more likely that they also

- Have become proficient in choice making/decision making by making conscious decisions in identifying preferred choices regarding living and working.

- Have succeeded in the process of goal setting and attainment, which involves long-range planning for seeking the education and training necessary for their chosen career.

- Exhibit an internal locus of control because they perceive a close relationship between their actions in terms of prerequisite training and preparation and employment and living outcomes.

- Have become more self-actualized to achieve their full potential by living in the community and working in their chosen careers.

- Can use self-advocacy to ensure access to the services and benefits needed to facilitate the achievement of this potential.

These assertions are supported by a follow-up study of students with cognitive or learning disabilities conducted by Wehmeyer and Schwartz (1997). They found that increased self-determination during high school years is linked to positive adult outcomes. Data were collected on students' self-determination prior to exiting high school and on adult outcomes 1 year after graduation. It was found that self-determined students were more likely to have achieved more positive adult outcomes, including being employed at a higher rate and having higher earnings than peers who were not as self-determined.

How Applicable Is Self-Determination for People with Severe Disabilities?

Self-determination is not a fixed concept. One does not reach a specific criterion and automatically become self-determined. It is a fluid concept, meaning that self-determination can (a) be different things to different people depending on their level of ability and interest and (b) be experienced at varying levels by the same individual throughout his or her lifetime. This concept lends itself to Brown's theory (Brown, Branston et al., 1979) of partial participation. It suggests that persons participate in activities related to self-determination to the maximum extent possible and that the support necessary for their participation be provided. A key principle is that the person with a disability maintains a degree of control over those activities. Not everyone will be able to participate in all aspects of self-determination. However, some aspect of self-determination is beneficial to everyone, regardless of the severity of physical or cognitive disabilities.

No matter what our physical and cognitive attributes, most of us have the ability to dream. Huven and Siegel (1995) challenged families, teachers, and adult service providers to give persons with all types of disabilities a chance to dream. The challenge is to offer everyone in this population every possible experience that will support future goals and dreams. Several self-determination programs (e.g., Field & Hoffman, 1996a; Lehman, 1996; New Hats, 1992;) have used dreams as the basis of activities that facilitate their actualization.

As mentioned in Chapter 1, self-advocacy is a key aspect of self-determination. Self-advocacy started as a civil rights movement by people with developmental disabilities—many of them with severe disabilities—who were rebelling against being underestimated, deprived of choices, treated like eternal children, and thought to lead lesser lives (Shapiro, 1993). Self-advocacy began in Sweden when Bengt Nirje, from his experience with children and adults with cognitive disabilities, came to the realization that they could and should have a role in their own choices (Shapiro, 1993). Self-advocacy and self-determination both grew out of Nirje's (1972) normalization principle and the resulting focus on dignity of risk. This principle requires "making available to the mentally retarded patterns and conditions of everyday life which are as close as possible to the norms and patterns of the mainstream of society" (Nirje, 1976, p. 363). Self-advocacy and self-determination in Nirje's conceptual framework provided people with severe disabilities choice and control (at least partially) within the norms and patterns of the mainstream.

When the Secondary Education and Transitional Services for Youths with Disabilities Program in the Office of Special Education and Rehabilitative Services (OSERS) supported a grant proposal competition to identify and teach skills necessary for self-determination, a total of 26 model demonstration projects were funded, including several focusing on cognitive and severe disabilities. Two projects (People First of Tennessee, Inc., 1991; People First of Washington, 1992) specifically targeted students with severe disabilities and adapted "People First" strategies for the adolescent population. Such strategies recognize and support people with developmental disabilities as full and capable citizens. They assist members to exercise the full rights and responsibilities of citizenship and to participate in the decisions that affect their lives and the lives of others. Most of the other projects developed a variety of activities and interventions for student populations with a range of disabilities.

How Does Cultural Diversity Influence Self-Determination?

There are several reasons why it is important to be aware of and address any conflicts related to self-determination that may be created by a discrepancy in cultural values. First, the ultimate purpose of self-determination is for students to intentionally create experiences in their lives that are consistent with their unique beliefs, needs, and preferences. Students' cultural backgrounds often have an important impact on those factors which make an individual unique (e.g., beliefs, interests) and need to be respected in any effort to help students express themselves more fully.

Second, environments and relationships, which are often influenced by cultural factors, have an important impact on the degree to which students will experience a sense of self-determination. For example, in interviews conducted with adolescents and adults with and without disabilities (Field, Hoffman, St. Peter, & Sawilowsky, 1992), the most frequently cited barrier to self-determination was "other people." In contrast, other people were also often identified as a significant support to becoming self-determined. The other people who were mentioned by the interview respondents were often family members. Self-determination instructional efforts need to help students negotiate environmental or relationship factors that are important to them. Cultural values often have an important effect on the environmental or relationship factors that influence self-determination. For example, Turnbull and Turnbull (1996) cited the comments of several Latin American parents from Argentina, Uruguay, and Brazil that reveal the tradition of family unity and permanence in their culture. These beliefs would likely have an impact on the way the concept of self-determination would be perceived by these families and the way in which self-determination would be expressed.

> "There is a relationship between parents and children that never breaks."

> "We never separate from our children, We never cut the cord."

> "It is against the family for the children to live alone as adults."

> "Young married couples live at their parents' home; it is Latino tradition."

> "Families live in the same house. . . . always has been that way." (p. 200)

Cultural background may also have a significant effect on the way in which students and their families interact with school personnel (Harry, 1992). For example, students and parents may be inhibited in their interactions with the school out of a cultural value of respect for authority and status or they may be alienated by the absence of personalism inherent in the formal system of documentation for special education.

The following guidelines are offered for considering and addressing the impact cultural factors have on self-determination for a particular student:

1. *Listen to the student and his or her family.*

   - Try to understand the influence that cultural background and values may have on the student's self-determination. Do not assume that just because students are members of a specific cultural group they or their parents adhere to certain beliefs. There is just as much variation among individuals within a culture as there is between cultures.

   - Seek to understand any discrepancies between the student and his or her parents related to cultural background and beliefs related to self-determination.

   - Keep in mind what self-determination may be in the context of the culture. Insignificant behavioral changes in one culture may be self-determination milestones in another.

2. *Strive to create "win-win" situations,*

- Aim to develop solutions whereby the needs of both the student and the parent are met and cultural values are respected.

The following examples demonstrate how cultural factors may influence self-determination and how those factors can be recognized and respected in a self-determination framework.

Cathy was a 16-year-old girl with a learning disability. An important component of her school program was preparation for employment and independent living. Her teacher found in talking with both her and her parents that, due to her religious background, her family expected that she would assume the role of wife and mother upon reaching adulthood and would not seek employment outside the home. Through discussion, the student, parent, and school staff agreed that Cathy should participate in work preparation classes so that (a) she would be prepared to work in case she did not marry and it became a necessary survival skill and (b) she would learn work habits that would be valuable in the home as well as in external work places.

John was a 17-year-old young man who was Native American. Within his culture, there was a strong belief that the importance of the group supersedes the individual and that the individual's primary purpose is to contribute to the group, not to advance oneself. John's teacher spent time with John and his parents to more fully understand his cultural heritage. As a result, John's self-determination instruction and support emphasized the following:

- When completing activities that helped to achieve greater self-awareness, John incorporated how his cultural heritage contributed to his sense of self.

- When developing individual goals, John developed goals that would help him make a greater contribution to group goals.

- The teacher included an activity for the entire class whereby the class established and worked toward a goal together to demonstrate how self-determination can be used to help groups be self-determined just as it can be used for individuals.

The whole point of self-determination is to help individuals fully express who they are and achieve goals that are important to them. Therefore, recognition and respect for cultural values is essential to successful self-determination efforts.

What Is the Role of Self-Determination in the General Education Curriculum?

Self-determination is important for students without disabilities just as it is for students with disabilities. There is substantial evidence supporting the notion that promoting self-determination for *all* youth could help them to (a) be more successful in their educational programs, (b) develop lifelong success skills, and (c) be protected from mental illnesses such as depression (Field, 1997). There are several ways in which a focus on self-determination can be incorporated within the general education curriculum.

First, several curriculum products promoting self-determination are appropriate for use in general education as well as special education. For example, *Project PARTnership* (Harris & McKinney, 1993), is a curriculum that promotes self-determination skills through arts activities. The curriculum provides several arts activities structured in a manner that supports self-awareness, goal setting, and self-expression. The curriculum also provides a process for structuring any arts activity so that important self-determination knowledge and skills are taught through the activity. *Project PARTnership* is just as appropriate for general education as it is for special education. *Steps to Self-Determination* (Field & Hoffman, 1996a) is a curriculum designed to be infused into general education or special education classes or to be delivered as an extracurricular activity. It has also been used in general education advisory or homeroom periods. The field-test of *Steps to Self-Determination* found no differences between students with and without disabilities related to their performance within the curriculum. *Take Action* (Martin Huber, Marshall, Maxson, & Hughes, in press) teaches a generalizable goal attainment process to all students and is designed for use in general education environments as well as in specialized settings.

A second way to promote self-determination in general education is to promote practices in the general education classroom that encourage and support self-determination. Examples of such practices include the following:

- Provide opportunities for choice on assignments.

- Have students in the class determine classroom rules within guidelines set by the teacher.

- Provide opportunities for students to set their own goals in the class.

- Allow students to monitor their own progress.

- Encourage "win-win" negotiations.

- Integrate class discussion related to self-determination principles in content activities.

A third way to promote self-determination in general education is through school-wide activities related to self-determination. The following are examples of school-wide practices that promote self-determination:

- Support strong, meaningful student government activities and provide opportunities for all students, including those with disabilities and those considered at risk, to be included in these activities.

- Provide for student choice in educational planning and scheduling.

- Provide an opportunity for student representatives to serve on school-wide committees.

- Develop disciplinary policies and practices that help students assess their choices.

- Focus student attention on role models who exhibit self-determination in the school community.

There is a wide range of ways in which self-determination can be supported throughout the school, from specific curricular efforts, to the way in which discipline is conducted, to the manner in which student scheduling is completed. Collaboration representing a variety of perspectives (e.g., students, parents, support services staff, special educators, general educators, and administrators) is needed to develop school-wide support for self-determination. It is important that change efforts aimed at bringing about increased self-determination be aligned with other reform initiatives affecting change in the schools, such as Goals 2000 and School to Work. The school improvement process provides one vehicle through which such planning can be accomplished.

What Supports Do Teachers and Administrators Need to Promote Self-Determination?

If we expect teachers and administrators to promote self-determination for youth, we must also encourage self-determination for teachers and administrators. Modeling is an effective instructional strategy (Bandura, 1986). Students will likely learn as much, if not more, about self-determination from what is modeled by school staff as from what is specifically taught in a curriculum. It will be exceedingly difficult, if not impossible, for school staff to promote youth self-determination if they do not experience a sense of self-determination themselves.

Field and Hoffman (1996b) identified key areas that need to be addressed to support educators in their efforts to be self-determined and to promote self-determination for their students. These are discussed in the following paragraphs.

Availability and Quality of Role Models for Staff. Just as students learn by observing models of self-determined behavior, so do teachers and administrators. Although models can be observed at all levels in the school environment, the models provided by those in key leadership positions are especially important. Does the superintendent provide an example of acting in an empowered manner, or does she complain that she is governed by the whims of the board or the community? Do parents speak up assertively for the rights of their children, or do they stay at home and remain passive? Factors such as these influence the degree to which self-determination is modeled as an important element in the school culture for teachers and students.

Examples of ways to consciously build in models for self-determination in the school environment follow.

1. Establish co-teaching teams in which teachers who have more experience with self- determination instructional efforts are paired with teachers who are less experienced in self-determination.

2. Develop policies and procedures that encourage and reinforce self-determination at all levels of the organization.

3. Use consultants and trainers who model self-determination for staff development activities.

Staff Curricular Issues. Self-determination is a relatively new concept in schools. Staff need the opportunity to learn about the concept of self-determination and how it fits into their lives and the lives of their students. Inservice training that (a) helps staff increase their own self-determination as well as that of their students and (b) looks at school-wide strategies as well as specific techniques or curricula will be most successful (Field & Hoffman, 1996b). The content of staff development to promote self-determination may include

- Introducing staff to the concept of self-determination and an understanding of the component skills.

- Providing staff with the opportunity to further develop component skills of self-determination (e.g., self-awareness, assertive communication, decision making, goal setting) for themselves.

- Providing an awareness of the instructional materials and strategies that are available to promote self-determination in students.

- Providing staff with support for addressing how self-determination can be infused into existing curricular efforts.

In addition to these recommendations for inservice training, staff will be better prepared to promote self-determination if their preservice preparation programs, at both the undergraduate and graduate levels, have provided a foundation for this effort. Preservice programs need to prepare students for the more consultative and less authoritarian roles that are consistent with self-determination. This orientation requires a major shift from traditional roles, and teachers need support for making this shift in their preparation programs. In addition, preservice programs need to offer multiple opportunities for students to listen to individuals from the population of persons with disabilities whom they are preparing to serve. Finally, teachers will be better prepared to promote self-determination if their self-determination has been encouraged in their educational programs. There is a need to examine personnel preparation programs and their course and fieldwork requirements, advising practices, instructional techniques, and methods of evaluation to determine whether their practices promote or discourage self-determination and make modifications as needed (Field & Hoffman, 1996b).

Opportunities for Choice. Just as students need opportunities for choice to exercise self-determination, so do school staff. They need to have opportunities to choose (a) to perform their jobs in a self-determined manner and (b) to promote self-determination for their students. A major factor affecting the degree to which teachers can promote self-determination is the level of control they have over the curriculum. If curriculum requirements are rigidly set, teachers will have difficulty finding ways to incorporate self-determination skills into the curriculum. In addition, if the system's bureaucracy is complex and inflexible, it will be difficult to introduce any new focus into the school. Policies that promote empowerment for staff and flexibility to respond to changing student needs will support teachers in their efforts to facilitate self-determination for their students.

Communication Patterns. The communication pattern in a school affects the degree to which students and staff feel encouraged to express themselves, initiate actions, and take risks. Staff communication patterns are typically expressed in three major areas: type of supervision, organizational structure, and reinforcement patterns (Field & Hoffman, 1996b). Examples of school communication patterns that promote self-determination are listed in Table 6-1.

How Should Self-Determination Instructional Programs Be Evaluated?

Evaluation of self-determination instructional programs should be undertaken as a collaborative process by all key persons involved in the self-determination instructional effort (e.g., students, parents, teachers, support staff and administrators). If evaluation of the program is to be effective, it is important that the evaluation process support the self-determination of all key parties as well as evaluate the effectiveness of the program. This team approach to evaluation is highly consistent with the team approach emphasized throughout transition programming. By considering the diverse perspectives of all key persons who are affected by the instructional program, an evaluation that is rich with information for program improvement can be obtained.

In addition to considering information from diverse perspectives, it is important to collect a variety of types of evaluation data. It is important to collect information that is subjective in nature (e.g., students', teachers', and parents' impressions, anecdotal information) as well as objective data

TABLE 6-1
Communication Patterns That Promote Self-Determination

Supervision	Organizational Structure	Reinforcement
• Establishing professional goals, performance indicators, and needed supports involves employees as active participants.	• Staff responsibilities and expectations are clearly understood.	• Staff accomplishments are acknowledged.
	• Decision making is participative.	• Attainment of goals established by the individual is rewarded.
• Performance appraisal process is a collaborative effort.	• Risk taking is encouraged.	
	• Communication lines are open.	

(e.g., pre- and posttest measures). Many different objectives can be met through the evaluation process, including (a) obtaining information for program improvement, (b) making decisions about how the program can best be delivered, and (c) reporting on the program to interested constituencies (e.g., school board, student and parent advisory groups). It is critical that participants be clear regarding the purpose of the evaluation process and that evaluation results be designed and used to meet that purpose. More detailed information about program evaluation can be found in Chapter 3, "Assessment of Self-Determination."

What Are Some of the Future Research and Development Needs in Self-Determination?

Although the focus on self-determination skills instruction has made a definitive imprint on the education of youth with disabilities, this initiative is still in its infancy, and to further its growth several research and development needs must be addressed. However, before looking forward, it may be helpful to examine the history of the self-determination initiative.

OSERS began this initiative in 1988 to focus on system-wide activities that would help people with disabilities have more input in the decisions that affect their lives (Ward & Kohler, 1996). An initial activity was to sponsor a National Conference in Washington, DC, to recommend activities to promote self-determination at the federal level. In response to one of the conference recommendations, the Secondary Education and Transitional Services for Youth with Disabilities Program within OSERS supported 26 model demonstration projects on self-determination during Fiscal Years 1990 through 1993. All of these projects were so successful in demonstrating the importance of self-determination that many proposals received under other competitions and proposals submitted under the State Systems for Transitional Services Program integrated a focus on self-determination. Even more extraordinary is that there are now many self-determination programs for youth with disabilities across the country that have not been involved with the federal initiative. Therefore, the spread of self-determination has exceeded expectations.

Despite the success of self-determination practices, some systems, programs, and services for persons with disabilities maintain a paternalistic, controlling, and demeaning approach in relating to their client-customers. Since most of these service providers rely on state and federal funds that are shrinking, such providers are looking for ways to provide their services as expeditiously as possible. The implementation of self-determination practices may correctly be viewed as requiring more time and energy. Therefore, the challenge is to first improve dissemination efforts on "best," proven, and promising practices that encourage youth with disabilities to take more control of their lives. These dissemination efforts need not only to target broad audiences, but also to facilitate the adoption of self-determination practices by making them easy to implement through responding to the general public's concerns and, perhaps, uneasiness. To do this, information must be disseminated that addresses self-determination in relation to the following:

- Agency downsizing.

- Maintenance of quality standards and appropriate classroom management.

- Availability of evaluation data on practice effectiveness.

- Buy-in by students, parents and other community members.

- Coordination with other reform initiatives such as Goals 2000 and School to Work.

- Modification of effective practices for specific disabilities.

Do We Know Everything There Is to Know About Self-Determination?

Considering that the history of the disability rights movement is about 30 years old, persons with disabilities have made great strides in securing opportunities for equal participation in society. Likewise, the efforts to teach skills necessary for self-determination to youth with disabilities only began with the 1988 federal initiative, but the lessons learned as to the importance of teaching these skills have been innumerable. Descriptions of such lessons appear elsewhere in this book; however, a few are worth highlighting.

The first lesson is that self-determination *is* important and that it needs to be addressed systematically through a specific curriculum. Preliminary data from the current self-determination effort have indicated that positive outcomes increased when students learn to make decisions, be assertive, and self-advocate (Ward & Kohler, 1996).

The second lesson is that it is imperative that youth with disabilities receive instruction in school to develop skills necessary for self-determination and that they have multiple opportunities to practice these skills (Ward & Kohler, 1996). Since many parents may have difficulty perceiving their youth with disabilities as empowered and self-determined adults, the cycle of dependency for too many of these youth will transfer from parents to teachers, job coaches, and welfare systems.

A third lesson is that self-determination skill instruction needs to begin with very young children. Since the federal projects focused on youth with disabilities who were approximately 14 to 21 years of age, there were reports that for some participants, 14 was far too late to reverse the cycle of dependency, learned helplessness, and feelings of inability. When asked how early self-determination instruction needed to start, project staff responded that it needed to begin right from infancy.

Many projects supported by the federal initiative expanded the parameters of the original concept of self-determination by focusing on diverse and cutting-edge issues (i.e., creativity, dream actualization, leadership). Many of us are amazed at the diversity and richness of the content and practices developed by the field during this short period of time. Yet, we also have the impression that we are still pushing the envelope in defining these parameters.

Issues such as leadership and empowerment *must* continue to be developed into a national and comprehensive instructional program for all persons with disabilities so that they can become a viable factor in our political culture. The lessons learned by other disenfranchised groups have not transferred to the population of persons with disabilities in terms of coalition building, the development of common vision and goals, and the use of en masse political clout as a means to an end. In an era of government cutbacks and downsizing, these issues will be increasingly important in ensuring that persons with disabilities remain part of the social fabric.

Some of these emerging issues may conflict with professional values (Field & Hoffman, 1996b). For example, what if, after being informed of all the benefits of being included in a general education class, a student (with input from his or her parents) chooses to remain in a more restrictive environment because that specific special education placement may offer good transition services necessary for ensuring successful postsecondary outcomes? The dilemma we face as professionals is whether our knowledge of the benefits of state-of-the-art practices such as inclusion should take precedence over an individual's right to choose what we may consider to be a less correct alternative. This alternative obviously has more personally relevant meaning, which may or may not be discernible to us. However, the sanctity of an individual's informed choice must be valued, and the issue must be resolved by the team, respecting the perspectives of each participant.

How Is Self-Determination Part of a Systems Change Movement?

In some cases, self-determination has already become integrated into the systems change movement. There has been sufficient impetus with the implementation of the provisions for consumer choice in the Rehabilitation Act Amendments of 1992 and transition requirements in the Individuals with Disabilities Education Act to help state and local systems to at least begin to address self-determination and consumer involvement issues. The Secondary Education and Transitional Services for Youth with Disabilities Program has supported 46 state systems change projects and has offered self-determination as one of the activities that could be supported by the grants. As stated elsewhere, this program has also funded 26 model demonstration self-determination projects, two research projects on student involvement in transition planning, and several outreach projects related to self-determination. Therefore, the federal effort is supporting the adoption of self-determination practices at the state level and also the replication of good models at the local level.

There is currently a school of thought that all discretionary programs funded through the Individuals with Disabilities Education Act should help states in their efforts to comply with Part B of the Act. States that had a compliance problem in a particular area (e.g., transition) would be able to "shop around" among projects engaged in research, model demonstration, outreach, and technical assistance on transition issues to help meet their compliance needs. Projects, in turn, would be required to somehow market and make available information, training, and/or technical assistance on what they have to offer to help with Part B compliance.

Self-determination programs can assist states in this effort, since the Part B regulations implementing the Individuals with Disabilities Education Act (IDEA) amendments pertaining to transition require that all students, beginning no later than age 16—and at a younger age if determined appropriate—be invited to attend the IEP meeting at which a transition plan is to be developed (*Federal Register*, October 22, 1997). IDEA further requires that transition services be based on an individual student's needs, taking into account the student's preferences and interests [Section 602(a)(19)]. Self-determination projects offer states interventions and strategies to help students identify their preferences and interests as well as taking an active, and often a leadership role in the IEP meeting.

Concomitant with the development of self-determination skills in individuals with disabilities, state policy and its implementation will have to change to create opportunities for self-determined behavior and support such behavior by individuals and groups. This is where the rubber meets the road. One track is to teach youth to be change agents, but if the system does not want to change, we had better also provide them with training in stress management. Therefore, it is necessary to move along a parallel track of developing systems that are ready, willing, and able to change and ready, willing, and able to support such change.

CONCLUSION

Much progress has been made in a short period of time to create supports and interventions that encourage self-determination for persons with disabilities in school settings. We have learned that we cannot expect students to develop the skills that lead to self-determination without specific, direct instruction. We have also learned that students will not develop or maintain these skills adequately if they are not given ample opportunities to practice them. Furthermore, we have found that it is important to begin self-determination skills instruction with very young children.

The self-determination movement has also raised many important questions and policy issues. Self-dtermination needs to be encouraged as part of a systems change movement. It needs to become an integral component of the foundation of our educational system, rather than an "add-on" partial effort. Self-determination skills need to be stressed throughout the educational program, and not just considered during transition planning. As such, they need to be a part of the general education program as well as the special education program. Finally, as part of a school-wide systemic approach to self-determination, we need to identify strategies to build and encourage self-determination for teachers and other school staff as well as for students.

REFERENCES

Bandura, A. (1986). *Social foundations of thought and action: A social cognitive theory.* Upper Saddle River, NJ: Prentice Hall.

Brown, L., Branston, M. B., Baumgart, D., Vincent, L., Falvey, M., & Schroeder, J. (1979). Using the characteristics of current and subsequent least restrictive environments as factors in the development of curricular content for severely handicapped students. *AAESPH Review, 4,* 407–424.

Federal Register, 62(204). (1997 Oct. 22). Proposed rules. Department of Education, 55025–55135.

Field, S. (1997). A historical perspective on student involvement in transition programs. *Career Development for Exceptional Individuals, 19*(2), 169–176.

Field, S., & Hoffman, A. (1996a). *Steps to self-determination.* Austin, TX: Pro-Ed.

Field, S., & Hoffman, A. (1996b). Increasing the ability of educators to promote youth self-determination. In L. E. Powers, G. H. S. Singer, & J. Sowers (Eds.), *Promoting self-competence among children and youth with disabilities: On the road to autonomy* (pp. 171–187). Baltimore: Paul H. Brookes.

Field, S., Hoffman, A., St. Peter, S., & Sawilowsky, S. (1992). *Skills and knowledge for self-determination: Interim research report.* Detroit: Wayne State University.

Harris, C., & McKinney, D. (1993). *Project partnership: Instructional kit.* Washington, DC: USA Educational Services.

Harry, B. (1992). *Cultural diversity, families and the special education system.* New York: Teachers College Press.

Hehir, T. (1994, April). *A national agenda for achieving better results for students with disabilities.* Paper presented at the spring leadership conference of the National Association of State Directors of Special Education.

Huven, R., & Siegel, S. (1995). Joining the community: Planning for adult life. In N. G. Haring & L. T. Romer (Eds.), *Welcoming students who are deaf-blind into typical classrooms: Facilitating school participation, learning and friendships.* (pp. 405–420). Baltimore: Paul H. Brookes.

Lehman, J. (1996). *Sharing the journey: An individual and integrated systems approach to self-determination.* Fort Collins: Colorado State University.

Martin, J., Huber Marshall, L., Maxson, L., & Hughes, W. (in press). *ChoiceMaker self-determination curriculum: Take action.* Longmont, CO: Sopris West.

New Hats, Inc. (1992). *It's my life project.* Salt Lake City: Author.

Nirje, B. (1972). The right to self-determination. In W. Wolfensberger (Ed.), *Normalization* (pp. 176–193). Toronto, Ontario, Canada: National Institute on Mental Retardation.

Nirje, B. (1976). The normalization principle and its human management implications. In M. Rosen, C. R. Clark, & M. S. Kivitz (Eds.), *The history of mental retardation: Collected papers* (Vol. 2, pp. 363–376). Baltimore: University Park Press.

People First of Tennessee, Inc. (1991). *Consumers helping students toward self-determination.* Nashville: Author.

People First of Washington. (1992). *Self-determination training for secondary students.* Clarkston, WA: Author.

Shapiro, J. P. (1993). *No pity: People with disabilities forging a new civil rights movement.* New York: Times Books.

Turnbull, A. P., & Turnbull, H. R. (1996). Self-determination within a culturally responsive family systems perspective: Balancing the family mobile. In L. E. Powers, G. H. S. Singer, & J. Sowers (Eds.), *Promoting self-competence among children and youth with disabilities: On the road to autonomy* (pp. 195–220). Baltimore: Paul H. Brookes.

Ward, M. J. (1988). The many facets of self-determination. *NICHCY transitions summary: National Information Center for Children and Youth with Disabilities, 5,* 2–3.

Ward, M. J., & Kohler, P. (1996). Teaching self-determination: Content and process. In L. E. Powers, G. H. S. Singer, & J. Sowers (Eds.), *Promoting self-competence among children and youth with disabilities: On the road to autonomy* (pp. 275–290). Baltimore: Paul H. Brookes.

Wehmeyer, M., & Schwartz, M. (1997). Self-determination and positive adult outcomes: A follow-up study of youth with mental retardation or learning disabilities. *Exceptional Children, 63,* 245–255.

APPENDIX

Self-Determination, Self-Advocacy, and Empowerment: An Annotated Bibliography

Abery, B., Rudrud, L., Arndt, K., Schauben, L., & Eggebeen, A. (1995). Evaluating a multi-component program for enhancing the self-determination of youth with disabilities. *Intervention in School and Clinic, 30*, 170–179. (ERIC Document Reproduction Service No. EJ 497 551)

In this article, the authors present the results of a study designed to serve as a preliminary evaluation of the effectiveness of a recently developed educational program to enhance the self-determination of young adults with mild disabilities. Participants in the study were 18 young adults with mental retardation. The purpose of the program was to provide these young adults with an opportunity to learn, practice, and refine skills, knowledge, and attitudes necessary for self-determination. The curriculum covered 10 topics: self-awareness, self-esteem, perceptions of personal control, personal values, goal setting, assertive communication, choice making, self-regulation, problem solving, and personal advocacy. The topics were taught over a 7-month period in 24 weekly sessions lasting 90 minutes. These sessions were implemented in small-group formats, mainly within family homes during times that were convenient for family members. One of the components evaluated in this program was the provision of education and instruction to families so they might better support their children's self-determination. The findings showed increased student involvement in a wide variety of family decisions.

Alper, S., Schloss, P. J., & Schloss, C. N. (1995). Families of children with disabilities in elementary and middle school: Advocacy models and strategies. *Exceptional Children, 62*, 261–270. (ERIC Document Reproduction Service No. EJ 513 604)

During the elementary and middle school years, the needs of the child with disabilities center on acquiring appropriate academic, social, community access, and self-management skills. Family members must work together with a wide array of educational and related services personnel on behalf of their child with a disability and, at the same time, care for the needs of all members of the family. This article describes models and methods of advocacy, including self-advocacy, social support advocacy, interpersonal advocacy, and legal advocacy. Particular emphasis is placed on advocacy strategies for individual family members of the child with the disabilities during the elementary and middle school years.

Balcazar, F. E., Seekins, T, Fawcett, S. B., & Hopkins, B. L. (1990). Empowering people with physical disabilities through advocacy skills training. *American Journal of Community Psychology, 18*(2), 281–295.

This 1990 study examines the impact of advocacy skills instruction to empower people with physical disabilities. Researchers monitored 14 group members and taught 6 members of an advocacy organization to identify and report disability-related issues at group meetings and to reach decisions on disability-related issues. The results illustrate increased group members' performance with service providers, overall improvement in the effectiveness of the consumer organization, and the value of longitudinal research with consumer organizations

Bramley, J., & Elkins, J. (1988). Some issues in the development of self-advocacy among persons with intellectual disabilities. *Australia and New Zealand Journal of Developmental Disabilities, 14*(2), 147–157. (ERIC Document Reproduction Service No. EJ 388 925)

A history of self-advocacy movements in Australia and the United States is highlighted in this article. The article focuses on individuals with intellectual disabilities in relation to self-advocacy. The problems of establishing and maintaining self-advocacy groups are addressed. Problems cited include (a) the need to redirect group members from advisors and toward one another, (b) maintaining interest and motivation, (c) poor concentration at group meetings, (d) members bringing personal conflicts to group meetings, (e) transportation problems that reduce attendance at meetings, and (f) dependence on the advisor to solve problems. Suggestions for ensuring the growth and quality of the self-advocacy movement in Australia are discussed.

Brinckerhoff, L. C. (1994). Developing effective self-advocacy skills in college-bound students with learning disabilities. *Intervention in School and Clinic, 29*(4), 229–237. (ERIC Document Reproduction Service No. EJ 479 477)

This article outlines and discusses the Summer Transition Program (STP), which is an orientation program for students with learning disabilities at Boston University. This program runs during the 6-week summer session and has three components: a 4-credit content course; learning strategies seminars; and topical workshops on using a computer, mastering a college library, and developing effective self-advocacy skills. Seminar sessions include (a) What Is Your Learning Disability in Plain Language?, (b) Legal Rights Under the Law, (c) Self-Advocacy, (d) Reasonable Accommodation in the Classroom, (e) Independence Versus Dependence Issues, (f) Strategy Instruction and Self-Advocacy Role Playing, and (g) Self-Advocacy Role Play and Direct Application. Differences between high school and college settings are also discussed.

Brinckerhoff, L. C., Shaw, S. F., & McGuire, J. M. (1992). Promoting access, accommodations and independence for college students with learning disabilities. *Journal of Learning Disabilities, 25,* 417–429. (ERIC Document Reproduction Services No. EJ 452 910)

This article focuses on the four primary issues that directly affect service delivery to students with learning disabilities in postsecondary settings: (1) How are high school and postsecondary settings different? (2) How are eligibility and access determined? (3) How are reasonable accommodations determined? and (4) How can the independence level of college students with learning disabilities be fostered? Each of these issues is discussed within the context of the student's transition from high school, including legal rights and responsibilities. Primary findings indicate that students (a) need to be taught study skills so they can study independently and (b) need to have more awareness of postsecondary expectations. To provide accessibility colleges must address students who have disabilities as individuals and not as a generic part of a group.

Brotherson, M. J., Cook, C. C., Cunconan-Lahr, R., & Wehmeyer, M. L. (1995). Policy supporting self-determination in the environments of children with disabilities. *Education and Training in Mental Retardation and Developmental Disabilities, 30*(1), 3–14. (ERIC Document Reproduction Service No. EJ 501 296)

This article examines the effects of environment on self-determination for individuals who have a disability. Opportunities to (a) learn skills of decision and choice making and (b) have an environment in which to practice these skills is necessary early in a child's life. Furthermore, these opportunities must exist in several of the child's environments to be effective. Legislation can make home, school, and community environments more equal in accessibility, which will promote self-determination skills. Children need to interact as much as possible in different physical environments in order to be self-determined adults. When physical environments are arranged with accessibility in mind, children with disabilities can feel more self-acceptance and higher self-esteem. The Americans with Disabilities Act, the Individuals with Disabilities Education Act, the Fair Housing Amendment Act, and the Rehabilitation Act are discussed as examples of legislation that can promote and make self-determination a reality for children and adults.

Bullock, C. C., & Mahon, M. J. (1992). Decision making in leisure: Empowerment for people with mental retardation. *Journal of Physical Education, Recreation, and Dance, 19,* 36–40. (ERIC Document Reproduction Service No. EJ 460 460)

The authors discuss the importance of instructing individuals with cognitive disabilities in decision-making skills in the areas of recreation and leisure. The authors suggest that such instruction can serve to empower these individuals and will enable society to perceive them as valuable and worthwhile members of the community. The authors present the DML (Decision Making in Leisure) model as a means for teaching decision making to individuals with cognitive disabilities. The DML model has four steps: (1) Identify a desired leisure experience, (2) Consider alternatives which satisfy the experience desired, (3) Describe the consequences for each alternative, and (4) Choose an alternative that satisfies the desired experience. The goal is that such instruction will generalize to settings outside the classroom and empower individuals to make choices on their own in a community setting.

Deci, E. L., & Chandler, C. L. (1986). The importance of motivation for the future of the learning disabilities field. *Journal of Learning Disabilities, 19,* 587–594. (ERIC Document Reproduction Service No. EJ 345 476)

In this article, the authors examine a series of papers on "The Future of the LD Field." They analyze and comment on the field's future from the perspective of Deci's distinguished work on human psychology. The result is a provocative discussion that first reviews the papers and then suggests that a key element missing in most of the presentations is the concept of human motivation. The authors offer a brief outline of basic psychological concepts not widely discussed in the LD field, such as emotional and motivational causes, and apply these concepts with regard to both treatment of learning disabilities and the process used to support and supervise the efforts of teachers. Self-determination is discussed as a goal of all education.

Deci, E. L., Connell, J. P., & Ryan, R. M. (1989). Self-determination in a work organization. *Journal of Applied Psychology, 74,* 580–590.

The authors review literature regarding self-determination, intrinsic motivation, leadership, and participative management. The authors emphasize that individuals experience behavior-regulating input as either "informational" or "controlling." Contingent rewards, deadlines, threats of punishment, evaluations, and surveillance are controlling and limit self-determination. Choice and positive feedback are informational and increase self-determination. Field studies of this framework indicate that three general factors are critical in facilitating self-determination: (1) support of autonomy, (2) noncontrolling positive feedback, and (3) acknowledgment of others' (employees' and/or subordinates') perspectives.

Durlak, C. M., Rose, E., & Bursuck, W. D. (1994). Preparing high school students with learning disabilities for the transition to postsecondary education: Teaching the skills of self-determination. *Journal of Learning Disabilities, 27*(1), 51–59. (ERIC Document Reproduction Service No. EJ 479 347)

This article summarizes a study designed to develop and implement an instructional program to teach self-determination skills to eight high school students with learning disabilities. Instructional procedures were adapted from direct instruction and learning strategies literature. The results suggest that students can acquire, maintain, and generalize skills that focus on the self-determination skills. The authors recommend that repeated practice of self-determination skills relating to self-awareness, self-advocacy, and assertiveness are essential if students with learning disabilities are to succeed in developing self-determination.

Field, S. (1996). Self-determination instructional strategies for youth with learning disabilities. *Journal of Learning Disabilities, 29*(1), 40–52. (ERIC Document Reproduction Service No. EJ 517 928)

This article describes four self-determination models, including (1) a model focused on individual beliefs, knowledge, and skills (Field & Hoffman, 1994); (2) a model based on self-determination as an adult outcome (Wehmeyer, 1992, in press); (3) a model based on self-regulation (Mithaug, Campeau, & Wolman, 1994); and (4) a model developed from an ecosystem perspective (Abery, 1994). Similarities and differences in these models are discussed. The author also examines current curricula and instructional strategies for self-determination. Instructional strategies include using modeling, providing opportunities for choice making, providing attribution retraining, and using appropriate behavioral strategies.

Field, S. & Hoffman, A. (1994). Development of a model for self-determination. *Career Development for Exceptional Individuals, 17*(2), 159–169. (ERIC Document Reproduction Service No. EJ 497 597)

The authors developed a model for self-determination and explained the steps they took in developing the model. The authors explain the model they developed and its five major components: (1) Know Yourself, (2) Value Yourself, (3) Plan, (4) Act, and (5) Experience Outcomes and Learn. The experience learned then adds to one's knowledge of self and one's values, and the process begins again. The model is intended for use with individuals with and without disabilities and can be used in an inclusive setting. This model is well researched and reviewed.

Ford, M. E. (1995). Motivation and competence development in special and remedial education. *Intervention in School and Clinic, 31*(2), 70–83. (ERIC Document Reproduction Service No. EJ 513 458)

This article explains the concept of motivation and how it can be applied to facilitate competence development. It discusses the importance of competence development and defines it as "the attainment of personally and socially valued goals and. . . progress toward those goals." The basic prerequisites for competence development are summarized as: It requires a person who is motivated, skillful, and biologically and functionally capable of facilitating relevant interactions within an environment in order to achieve specific goals.

Foxx, R. M., Faw, G. D., Taylor, S., Davis, P. K., & Fulia, R. (1993). "Would I be able to. . . ?" Teaching clients to assess the availability of their community living life style preferences. *American Journal on Mental Retardation, 98*, 235–48. (ERIC Document Reproduction Service No. EJ 470 715)

This study examines a three-phase program used to assist six institutionalized adults with mild cognitive disabilities in their transition to community living. In phase one, an interview format was used to assess the clients' choice-making skills concerning their own life-style preferences. Phase two was used to identify the clients' strongest life-style preferences. Photos were used to determine what each client had a greater preference for (e.g., photos depicting a separate shower/toilet or multiple shower/toilets). The purpose of phase three was to evaluate the program to teach clients to assess themselves regarding the availability of their life-style choices during tours of group homes and report back to their social worker. The findings highlight the importance of ensuring that clients are actively involved in their own placement process. They needed to be instructed in the questioning process because they had not perceived that choices were available to them or that their input was being sought.

Gould, M., & McTaggart, N. (1988–89, Winter). Self-advocacy for transition: Indications of student leadership potential today. *American Rehabilitation*, pp. 16–24.

This article describes a study of 13 students ages 17 to 21 who participated in a transition planning study. These students had participated in 7 months of self-advocacy instruction prior to the study. The article describes group goals of the young adults and specifies those that were related to student-identified transition issues. The study illustrates how a group of young adults with disabilities can work together and assume responsibility for their transition from school to adult life.

Halpern, A. S. (1994). The transition of youth with disabilities to adult life: A position statement of the Division on Career Development. *Career Development for Exceptional Individuals*, *17*, 115–124. (ERIC Document Reproduction No. EJ 497 593)

The author reviews the historical evolution of the definition of transition and summarizes the current concept adopted by the Division on Career Development and Transition. The author suggests that attention be focused on four components of the transition plan: (1) an emerging sense of student empowerment, which eventually enhances student self-determination within the transition planning process; (2) student self-evaluation as a foundation for transition planning; (3) student identification of postsecondary goals that are consistent with the outcomes of their self-evaluation; and (4) student selection of appropriate educational experiences to pursue during high school that are consistent with aspirations and postschool goals. The author also outlines considerations to be addressed before selecting a model of delivery for transition services.

Hoffman A., & Field, S. (1995). Promoting self-determination through effective curriculum development. *Intervention in School and Clinic*, *30*, 134–141. (ERIC Document Reproduction Service No. EJ 497 546)

Authors take the self-determination model published in 1994 and apply it to curriculum development. They explain the self-determination model and describe the 10 cornerstones to guide the design of using the self-determination model as a basis for curriculum development. These cornerstones include (1) teachers are co-learners; (2) modeling; (3) cooperative learning; (4) experiential learning; (5) inclusive instruction; (6) family/friend participation and support; (7) the power of listening; (8) team teaching; (9) humor; and (10) teachable moments. The outline of a 16-week curriculum was provided. Six assessment tools were developed to measure cognitive, behavioral, and affective domains. Two instruments were used as pre- and posttests to assess curriculum effectiveness. The model has demonstrated much promise.

Houghton, J. Bronicki, G. J. B., & Guess, D. (1987). Opportunities to express preferences and make choices among students with severe disabilities in classroom settings. *The Journal of the Association for Persons with Severe Handicaps*, *12*, 18–27. (ERIC Document Reproduction Service No. EJ 354 015)

Observers recorded opportunities to express preferences and make choices in classrooms for students with severe disabilities. The code included condition (structured vs. unstructured), communicative intent (choice or preference), initiations by type, and responses by type and amount. Staff-initiated opportunities for student expressions of choice or preference were significantly higher in the age range 0 to 5. Regardless of age range or setting, staff responded to student initiations infrequently. Less structure was associated with low rates of responsiveness to students.

Hoy, C. (1986). Preventing learned helplessness. *Academic Therapy, 22*(1), 11–18. (ERIC Document Reproduction Service No. EJ 341 266)

The author examines practices that foster learned helplessness in students with learning disabilities. The author discusses the ramifications of learned helplessness along with suggested steps to overcoming and avoiding the pitfalls of learned helplessness. The steps are designed for student use. There are also suggestions for teachers to assist students in avoiding learned helplessness. Some of these steps include allowing students input and a sense of responsibility, modeling responses to success and failure, setting goals, and solving problems.

Hughes, C. A., Korinek, L., & Gorman, J. (1991). Self-management for students with mental retardation in public settings: A research review. *Education and Training in Mental Retardation, 26*, 271–291. (ERIC Document Reproduction Service No. EJ 434 549)

This article is an analysis of 19 data-based studies regarding self-management procedures published in the literature between January, 1970, and January, 1989, regarding students with cognitive disabilities in the public school setting. All 19 studies reported at least partial positive results of self-management instruction with students who have cognitive disabilities. Results indicated that youngsters with cognitive disabilities can benefit from self-management instruction. Evidence of generalization was found in the limited number of studies that conducted testing for generalization. The authors suggest that further research is needed to answer questions regarding specific student characteristics and behaviors that are most likely amenable to self-management procedures, the components of a self-management instruction program, and maintenance and generalization strategies.

Ingram, R. (1988). Empower. *Social Policy, 19*(2), 11–16.

This article explores self-advocacy as it relates to recipients of welfare benefits. In confronting problems and concerns within a group setting, individuals empower themselves and each other as they collectively face a system that devalues their worth in society. The author suggests that a group leader must model a position of power through assertiveness and knowledge of the welfare system to group members. Empowerment is a process reinforced by other recipient members and results in increased self-respect.

Institute on Community Integration (1993/1994). Feature issue on self-determination. *Impact, 6*(4), 1–20.

This special issue explores the relevance of self-determination for persons with developmental disabilities across the lifespan, ways to express self-determination, and obstacles to implementation. Topics include Self-Determination and Young Children (Abery, 1993; Eggebeen & Leigh, 1993; Mendenball & McBride, 1993); Self-Determination for School-Age Children (Doyle, York, & Kronberg, 1993; Ward, 1993; Wehmeyer, 1993); Self-Determination During the Transition Age (Beckwith, 1993; Thompson & Corbey, 1993); and Self-Determination During Adulthood (Sajevic, 1993; West, Kregel, & Revell, 1993). Specific topics include families and self-determination, early interventions, transition, and guardianship and self-determination.

Izzo, M. V., Pritz, S. G., & Ott, P. (1990). Teaching problem solving skills: A ticket to a brighter future. *The Journal for Vocational Special Needs Education, 13*(1), 23–26. (ERIC Document Reproduction Service No. EJ 419 517)

This article discusses the importance of teaching problem-solving skills to all students, including those with disabilities. The authors give a rationale for teaching this important skill by emphasizing change in the work place. Jobs requiring minimal skills are disappearing, and workers are being required to reason and solve problems regardless of their job title. The authors believe that this skill area should be a fundamental part of the curriculum in our schools, and they describe a four-step process for problem solving, selecting materials, and providing a positive environment for use in the classroom. The four steps are as follows: (1) state the problem, (2) list the choices that are available, (3) identify the consequences of each choice, and (4) select the choice that best meets immediate as well as long-term needs.

Kishi, G., Teelucksingh, B., Zollers, N., Park-Lee, S., & Meyer, L. (1988). Daily decision-making in community residences: A social comparison of adults with and without mental retardation. *American Journal on Mental Retardation, 92*, 430–435. (ERIC Document Reproduction Service No. EJ 370 379)

Researchers interviewed adults with cognitive disabilities living in community group homes (*n* = 24) and adults without cognitive disabilities living independently (*n* = 42) and assessed their daily decision making on a 10-item survey. Group home residents reported less opportunity for decision making than the group without cognitive disabilities on 8 of 10 survey items. These 8 items included (1) what to eat, (2) what activities to engage in during free time, (3) who to live with, (4) whether to make a social phone call, (5) whether to stay up late or go to bed early, (6) what job or work to do, (7) what TV show to watch, and (8) how to spend money not committed for expenses. The authors suggest that professionals must work harder to secure personal autonomy, freedom, and choice for persons with cognitive disabilities.

Kohn, A. (1993). Choices for children: Why and how to let students decide. *Phi Delta Kappan, 75*(1), 8–20. (ERIC Document Reproduction Service No. EJ 470 490)

One of the worst side effects of the traditional approach to teaching is the burnout of students. Just as teachers and other adults in a variety of jobs burn out over time, so do children, even as young as elementary age. This is due in large part to the lack of opportunity for involvement in the decision-making processes of their academic matters and other aspects of school. This article discusses the lack of self-determination as a cause of burnout and misbehavior. The author also provides a wide range of practices for teachers to use to engage students in making decisions regarding their education.

Lewis, K., & Taymans, J. (1992). An examination of autonomous functioning skills of adolescents with learning disabilities. *Career Development for Exceptional Individuals, 15*, 37–46. (ERIC Document Reproduction Service No. EJ 449 989)

Students with learning disabilities frequently fail to exhibit important behaviors that are indicative of autonomy, such as successful employment and separation from parents. The purpose of this study was to find out whether or not there were large differences between the autonomous functioning of adolescents with or without learning disabilities (LD). They studied 100 families who had adolescents with LD between the ages of 14 and 18, with one parent rating her or his child's autonomous functioning. The Autonomous Functioning Checklist was used as a measurement tool. The results indicated a significant difference in the use of community resources and in self-management of the adolescents with LD. The authors indicate that independent living instruction may be vital in developing autonomy in students with LD. The authors agree that more research is needed to adequately service the needs of adolescents with LD.

Ludi, D. C., & Martin, L. (1995). The road to personal freedom: Self-determination. *Intervention in School and Clinic, 30*(3), 164–169. (ERIC Document Reproduction Service No. EJ 497 550)

In this article the authors introduce a self-determination curriculum that has been piloted with students from different ethnic backgrounds with mild, moderate, and severe disabilities. The article defines self-determination, examines selected research, and introduces the reader to an overview of the curriculum designed by the authors. The authors provide teacher and trainer tips for addressing self-determination. The tips include (a) use language that identifies a student as a person and not a disability, (b) help students accept their disabilities, (c) encourage interdependence with each other and community, (d) educate parents, and (e) provide teachers with support mechanisms that result in improved teaching skills.

Martin, J. E., & Marshall, L. H. (1995). ChoiceMaker: A comprehensive self-determination transition program. *Intervention in School and Clinic, 30*, 147–156. (ERIC Document Reproduction Service No. EJ 497 548)

This article discusses the Choicemaker Self-Determination Transition Program. With the use of this model, students learn to choose goals, express goals, and take action while addressing six areas of transition planning. The six areas include post-high-school education, employment, personal recreation and leisure, housing and daily living, community participation, and high school interest. The program includes a curriculum component and an assessment component that can be used to document student needs and assess program achievement across time.

Martin, J. E., Marshall, L. H., & Maxson, L. M. (1993). Transition policy: Infusing self-determination and self-advocacy into transition programs. *Career Development for Exceptional Individuals*, *16*(1), 53–61. (ERIC Document Reproduction Service No. EJ 465 409)

Special education students are poorly equipped to assess their needs, set goals, plan actions, act, monitor progress, and make adjustments when they leave special education programs. The IEP and transition processes are experiences in which the student can take a direct role and learn the skills of self-determination and self-advocacy. This article discusses the transition law, the IEP purpose, changes that need to be made, and The Adaptability Model (Mithaug, 1987) used in Colorado Springs to teach self-management and self-advocacy skills.

Martin, J. E., Oliphint, J. H., & Weisenstein, G. R. (1994). ChoiceMaker: Transitioning self-determined youth. *Rural Special Education Quarterly*, *13*(1), 16–23. (ERIC Document Reproduction Service No. EJ 482 190)

The authors of this article correlate success with being self-determined. A group of successful adults with learning disabilities were interviewed and the results showed that they had, among other characteristics, persistence, well-thought-out goals, and a desire to succeed. One of the ways to make students with learning disabilities more successful is to have them be active in their IEP planning process. The authors suggest using a "choose, manage, evaluate, and adjust" model to empower students with LD so that they are able to make and implement their own decisions. This is called the Self-Directed Employment Program, which has three phases: assessment, placement, and follow-up. Long-term vocational success is correlated with a job that matches preferences and skills, not disability categories.

Miller, R. J. (1994). Preparing for adult life: Teaching students their rights and responsibilities. *CEC Today*, *1*(7), 12.

The author suggests that time in the educational curriculum must be spent on teaching students to understand their rights and responsibilities under the law. Students must learn to discuss their educational strengths and limitations if they are to get what they need and want. These skills are fundamental to self-advocacy. The goal of education is to develop self-directed learners who can address their own wants and concerns and can advocate for their goals and aspirations.

Miller, R. J., Corbey, S., & Asher, G. (1994). Promoting postsecondary education for high school-aged youth with disabilities: A model of empowerment. *Rural Special Education Quarterly*, *13*(1), 57–63. (ERIC Document Reproduction Service No. EJ 482 196)

This article summarizes a 1-day conference designed to bring together students with disabilities who had been successful in postsecondary education, representatives of technical colleges, community colleges, and universities and 156 secondary-age students with disabilities who wanted to find out more about their participation in postsecondary education. Pre- and posttesting of student participants found that after attending the conference: (a) students increased in their perceived ability to describe the educational impact of their disability to someone else; (b) students increased in their perception of their ability to describe classroom accommodations they would need in postsecondary education; (c) students increased in their understanding of how to access financial assistance to attend postsecondary education; and (d) students increased in the likelihood that they would self-identify themselves as a person with a disability to get the services they deserved in postsecondary education.

Miller R. J., Corbey, S., & Springs Doss, R. L. (1994). Promoting postsecondary education for high school-aged youth with disabilities: Influencing teacher attitudes, developing teacher knowledge. *Issues in Special Education and Rehabilitation. 9*(1), 69–78.

This article discusses a study done to measure the effect of participation in a state-wide conference regarding young adults with disabilities in postsecondary education on educational personnel. The purpose of the study was to determine changes in knowledge and attitudes that occurred in special education teachers and support staff as a result of participation in the conference. After participation in the conference, educators were more likely to perceive the importance of including postsecondary education as a portion of their students' IEPs. Educators increased in their knowledge of skills needed by students to be successful in postsecondary education. They also became more aware of the support services available to students in postsecondary settings.

Mitchell, B. (1988). Who chooses? *National Information Center for Handicapped Children and Youth with Handicaps: Transition Issues, 5,* 4–5.

In this article, the author challenges professionals and others to provide more opportunities for children with disabilities to make choices for themselves and to help each child to cope with the consequences of his or her choices. Persons with disabilities must be provided opportunities to explore their capabilities and options. Common barriers that restrict self-determination include overprotection, low expectations, and a lack of stable support systems that promote feelings of security and enhance coping skills.

Mithaug, D. E. (1991). *Self-determined kids.* Lexington, MA: Lexington Books.

In this book the author examines self-determination and its effects on the success and failure of children. The author contends that children who succeed are self-directed and self-correcting in order to meet and exceed expectations and goals. The roles of intelligence, competence, and persistence are explored as principles of success and self-determination for youth. The author's competency principle suggests that the greater the competence of the individual, the more positive the results. The greater the self-confidence, the move positive the self-esteem. Intelligence is the second principle of self-determination. Successful people are intelligent adaptors. Self-determined youth maximize the matches between their likes and what they can do. These individuals harness intrinsic motivation with natural ability. They match results and evaluation and continually adjust and fine tune their adaptive fit to maximize their opportunities. The final principle of self-determination is persistence. The more persistent the individual is in solving problems, the more likely it is that the individual will achieve the desired goal. The author also explores the attitudes of some youth that they are entitled to the good life.

Ness, J. E. (1989). The high jump: Transition issues of learning disabled students and their parents. *Academic Therapy, 25*(1), 33–40. (ERIC Document Reproduction Service No. EJ 400 608)

Students with learning disabilities and their parents may be involved in some dramatic and stressful changes in their normal routine when facing the possibility of transition from a secondary to a postsecondary setting. It is important for special education professionals to be aware of the problems students with learning disabilities and their parents encounter during the transition process. This article explains some of the issues that face students with learning disabilities and their parents during this difficult period. With a team approach of teachers, students, parents, and counselors cooperating to make a plan, the transition can be made much easier.

O'Brien, J. (Ed.). (1990). *Effective self advocacy: Empowering people with disabilities to speak for themselves.* Minneapolis: Institute on Community Integration, University of Minnesota.

This monograph was based on a workshop designed to assist people with developmental disabilities to speak for themselves. Eighteen individuals from seven states with extensive experience in developing self-advocacy groups discussed several issues, including (a) What works to help people speak for themselves and to change their own lives? (b) What works to assist people to speak out to change conditions for all persons with disabilities? and (c) What will strengthen self-advocacy? Responses dealt with issues such as becoming politically active, influencing the media, empowerment, and the development and support of local self-advocacy chapters.

Phillips, P. (1990). A self-advocacy plan for high school students with learning disabilities: A comparative case study analysis of student's, teacher's, and parents' perceptions of program effects. *Journal of Learning Disabilities, 23,* 466–471. (ERIC Document Reproduction Service No. EJ 420 071)

This article reports on a study of students with learning disabilities in a comprehensive high school and the effects of a self-advocacy program as perceived by the students, parents, and resource teachers. The program was a 10-week seminar in learning disabilities which met once per week under the leadership of a counselor and a resource teacher. Topics discussed included (1) the concept of a learning disability; (2) information about specific learning disabilities; (3) school and social relation issues that relate to learning disabilities; (4) specific learning strengths and weaknesses of participating students; (5) people who have learning disabilities and have succeeded in careers; (6) legislation; (7) availability of postsecondary education assistance; and (8) the responsibilities of Division of Rehabilitation Services. The author suggests that the self-advocacy plan is an effective program for increasing student awareness of services they qualify for, clarifying their perceptions as learners with LD, increasing their understanding of LD and its characteristics, and developing an awareness of career and educational opportunities.

Realon, R. E., Favell, J. E., & Lowerre, A. (1990). The effects of making choices on engagement levels with persons who are profoundly multiply handicapped. *Education and Training in Mental Retardation, 25,* 299–305. (ERIC Document Reproduction Service No. EJ 419 994)

The purpose of this study was to evaluate the use of choice making for individuals with profound disabilities. The participants in this study were two adults with profound disabilities who had a variety of mental, social, and physical deficits. The study was conducted in a residential setting. The conclusions suggested that choice making did impact the amount of interaction by study participants. The authors also discussed the possibility of using these results in programming in other areas.

Renzulli, J. S., & Reis, S. M. (1991). Building advocacy through program design, student productivity and public relations. *Gifted Child Quarterly, 35,* 182–187. (ERIC Document Reproduction Service No. EJ 439 633)

This article discusses the idea that building advocacy for serving students should be a priority for all persons working in these programs. It introduces the process of building advocacy through the program itself, the progress of participating students, and the continued commitment of public relations. The article identifies factors common to programs that have survived the budget cuts and financial crisis, especially in the New England states.

Rhoades, C. M., Browning, P. L., & Thorin, E. J. (1986). Self-help advocacy movement: A promising peer-support system for people with mental disabilities. *Rehabilitation Literature, 47*(1–2), 2–7. (ERIC Document Reproduction Service No. EJ 333 149)

This article presents a history of the self-advocacy movement for persons with cognitive disabilities and other developmental disabilities, which started in the 1960s and 1970s with other civil rights movements. It was referred to as a "quiet revolution." The group began in Oregon in 1973, and by the end of the decade had over 5,000 members. Now there is an international network of self-help advocacy groups. The authors state that individuals with developmental disabilities who have friendships and peer support are more socially satisfied than those who do not. They also explore the social stigma associated with being labeled mentally retarded. The self-help groups recognize the importance of a nonpeer participant such as an advisor to help facilitate the group. This advisor gives support and encouragement in a nonauthoritarian way. Many people find strength and acceptance in self-help groups.

Roffman, A. J. , Herzog, J. E., & Wershba-Gershon, P. M. (1994). Helping young adults understand their learning disabilities. *Journal of Learning Disabilities, 27,* 413–419. (ERIC Document Reproduction Service No. EJ 487 998)

This study evaluated the effectiveness of the *Understanding Learning Disabilities* (ULD) course designed to promote self-advocacy and self-awareness in young adults with learning disabilities functioning in the low average intellectual range. The Threshold curriculum was designed to prepare young adults to become independent, responsible, and productive citizens. The

Threshold curriculum is a 2-year comprehensive program that includes vocational preparation for paraprofessional positions in human services and clerical settings, independent living instruction, social skills instruction, and practical academics. Results of ANOVAs performed on posttest questionnaire and interview scores support the effectiveness of the ULD course in expanding students' knowledge base regarding their learning disabilities and teaching them to apply self-understanding in a social context. Significant correlates of ULD performance included IQ, academic achievement, and vocational functioning.

Salembier, G., & Furney, K. S. (1994). Promoting self-advocacy and family participation in transition planning. *The Journal for Vocational Special Needs Education, 17*(1), 12–17. (ERIC Document Reproduction Service No. EJ 494 239)

This article explores a model that promotes the concept of self-advocacy and a student and family approach to planning known as the McGill Action Planning System (MAPS). The approach brings together a team of people to brainstorm ideas and answer questions concerning an individual's history, dreams, fears, characteristics, and current and future needs. The information is used to identify goals and develop a plan for the future that includes ongoing support for the individual.

Schloss, P., Alpers, S., & Jayne, D. (1994). Self-determination for persons with disabilities: Choice, risk, and dignity. *Exceptional Children, 60*(3), 215–225. (ERIC Document Reproduction Service No. EJ 474 392)

Follow-up studies indicate that the majority of special education graduates have not made a successful transition from high school to the adult world. This article gives statistics related to employment and postsecondary education rates, discusses the importance of self-determination, and explains the choice continuum for individuals and assessment information needed to assist in teaching self-determination skills. Assessment ideas include interviewing parents and other professionals, interviewing the student, and direct observation of the student.

Serna, L. A. (1995). Teaching self-determination skills to adolescents. *Intervention in School and Clinic, 30*, 132–133.

Many adolescents are unable to make career and life decisions for themselves. They are unable to guide themselves and take an active part in determining what is to happen in their future.

To change this, a curriculum that facilitates self-determination among adolescents must be developed and used. Some general concepts include learning about their environment and making personal choices based on this knowledge. The students should also consider how their decisions will have an impact on the lives of others. The self-determined student also demonstrates social skills, decision or choice making, and goal setting.

Curriculum changes must include (a) teaching students how to become responsible for their learning, (b) changing teachers' approaches to classroom instruction, (c) providing strategies for teachers and students to collaborate with one another toward more effective learning, and (d) preparing families to plan for the future.

Serna, L. S., & Lau-Smith, J. A. (1995). Learning with purpose: Self-determination skills for students who are at risk for school and community failure. *Intervention in School and Clinic, 30,* 142–146. (ERIC Document Reproduction Service No. EJ 497 547)

The number of youths at risk in schools and communities has reached critical proportions. This article outlines a self-determination curriculum designed to enhance the skills of students at risk for failure. The authors explain how they developed their list of self-determination skills and defined self-determination. The authors describe the curriculum and introduce a parent component. Curriculum components include (a) social skills, (b) self-evaluation skills, (c) self-direction skills, (d) networking skills, (e) collaboration skills, (f) persistence and risk-taking skills, and (g) the skills to deal with stress. The article provides a detailed comparison of successful and at-risk behaviors and explains how the curriculum meets the needs of students who are at risk.

Siever, A. L., Cuvo, A. J., & Davis, P. K. (1988). Training self-advocacy skills to adults with mild handicaps. *Journal of Applied Behavior Analysis, 21,* 299–309. (ERIC Document Reproduction Service No. EJ 380 181)

Researchers developed an instructional program designed to teach adults with mild disabilities self-advocacy skills. The study involved eight participants ranging in age from 19 to 27 years. Using teaching methods involving role-play situations, four general rights categories were addressed. Instruction was offered to teach whether or not basic legal rights were violated in certain interpersonal situations, and then instruction in the steps to a general complaint process was provided. Participants learned to discriminate and respond to over 200 hypothetical interpersonal situations. These participants were also able to learn the proper complaint process. Concerns about generalization are discussed.

St. Peter, S., Field, S., Hoffman, A., & Keena V. (1992). Self-determination: An annotated bibliography. Detroit: Wayne State University.

The authors provide a sampling of the professional literature regarding self-determination. The literature review is organized under descriptors that include self-determination, self-advocacy, self-esteem, self-efficacy, assertiveness, choice-making, self-concept, control, independence/interdependence, competence, and creativity.

Szymanski, E. M. (1994). Transition: Life-span and life-space considerations for empowerment. *Exceptional Children, 60,* 402–410. (ERIC Document Reproduction Service No. EJ 479 466)

The author discusses the life-span and life-space considerations of the transition process. The foundation for transition begins in the early childhood years and should involve not only the individual student, but his or her family and community as well. It is also important to consider the influence of cultural background when planning interventions and setting goals. The author outlines four principles of intervention for professionals to consider during transition planning so that the process may serve as an empowering experience for the student, family, and community. These four principals include (1) interventions should be designed to be maximally under the control of the individual rather than others, (2) interventions should facilitate individual autonomy, (3) the least intrusive means that are still effective should be used, and (4) the most natural interventions for the particular work environment should be used.

Thorin, E. (1988). Measuring knowledge of citizenship rights and responsibilities. *Research in Developmental Disabilities, 9*(1), 85–92. (ERIC Document Reproduction Service No. EJ 368 877)

This study focused on developing an instrument to assess the knowledge that people with cognitive disabilities have of their citizenship rights and responsibilities. The test development phase included generating 83 items in six content areas including human, civil, and legal rights and moral, civic, and legal responsibilities. The test was pilot tested with 236 members of self-advocacy groups for persons with developmental disabilities. The resulting 30-item, true-false formatted instrument was standardized with a sample of 391 self-advocates from 13 states. The psychometric properties of the Rights and Responsibilities Instrument supported its potential use as a screening, diagnosis, and program evaluation tool.

Valenti, R. A. (1989). *Developing self-advocacy: A practical guide and workbook for preparing high school learning disabled students and their parents.* Columbia, MO: Hawthorne Educational Services.

This material was designed by the author as a practical guide and workbook for preparing high school students with learning disabilities for postschool success. Topics include: (a) understanding specific learning disabilities, (b) understanding diagnostic testing, (c) knowing your rights and responsibilities under the law, (d) understanding the transition process to postsecondary education, and (e) developing skills for independent learning.

Van Reusen, A. K., & Bos, C. B. (1990). I-PLAN: Helping students communicate in planning conferences. *TEACHING Exceptional Children, 22* (4), 30–31. (ERIC Document Reproduction Service No. EJ 410 369)

Student involvement in the IEP planning conference is for the most part either nonexistent or passive. Providing students with a strategy and opportunities for participating in decision-making conferences could have an immediate effect on their involvement and communication in determining their educational goals. The education planning strategy is an effective way to assist students in assuming active roles in the educational decision-making process. Students learn to use a strategy that focuses on effective planning and communication. Students learn to use the acronym I-PLAN to remember the following five steps in the IEP process: I-Inventory your strengths, weaknesses, needs, and preferences; P-Provide your inventory information; L-Listen; A-Ask questions; and N-Name your goals. Such involvement encourages self-determination and empowers students by giving them opportunities to make decisions and take responsibility concerning their needs and, more important, their futures.

Van Reusen, A. K., & Bos, C. B. (1994). Facilitating student participation in individualized education programs through motivation strategy instruction. *Exceptional Children, 60,* 466–475. (ERIC Document Reproduction Service No. EJ 479 472)

This article investigates the success of teaching high school students with learning disabilities to be active participants in the IEP conference by providing instruction and practice prior to the IEP conference. The authors recommend that with sufficient instruction students with learning disabilities can lead their IEP meetings. The focus of this strategy is on student motivation, communication, and self-advocacy. All of these components are necessary for successful transition from school to adult life.

Varela, R. A. (1988). Self-determination and normalization among adolescents: The family as a crucible of values. *National Information Center for Handicapped Children and Youth with Handicaps: Transition Issues, 5,* 6–7.

Parent advocacy is an important component in the self-determination of adolescents with disabilities. If adolescents are to realize their potentials, they must gradually increase their levels of independent planning and decision making. Inevitable parent-child conflicts arise with widening social circles and increased decision making. Models of how families deal with these conflicts are discussed.

Ward, M. (1988). The many facets of self-determination. *National Information Center for Handicapped Children and Youth with Handicaps: Transition Issues, 5,* 2–3.

Self-determination involves at least the following: self-actualization, assertiveness, creativity, pride, and self-advocacy. Adolescence is a critical time for self-determination as young persons challenge parental authority, assert independence, and increase control over their own lives. Parents often have difficulty providing adolescents with disabilities opportunities for making decisions and for making contributions to the household (e.g., chores). Perhaps most important, adolescents with disabilities are provided few opportunities for growth acquired through failure.

Ward, M. (1991). Self-determination revisited: Going beyond expectations. *National Information Center for Handicapped Children and Youth with Handicaps: Transition Summary, 7,* 3–5.

This article briefly defines self-determination and emphasizes that personal characteristics that lead to self-determination develop gradually and begin in early childhood. Examples of simple decision-making skills, ways of encouragement, and barriers to these skills are given. Attitude toward a disability or the child with the disability as well as financial obstacles are seen as detrimental to independence and self-determination. With emphasis on the role of parents in assisting children to become more independent, two processes for involving the child in his or her environment are discussed. Suggestions are also made to help children see themselves positively despite the disability. Suggestions for parents and teachers include: (a) Be honest about the disability, (b) avoid negative terms such as *hardship* and *burden*, (c) avoid comparisons with others, and (d) stress positive coping strategies.

Wehmeyer, M. L. (1992a). Self-determination and the education of students with mental retardation. *Education and Training in Mental Retardation, 27,* 302–314.

Self-determination is "the capacity to choose and to have those choices be the determinants of one's actions." This is not always the reality for individuals with cognitive disabilities. The article discusses educating learners with cognitive disabilities about the importance of self-determination. Implications relevant to student achievement are given, as well as implications for special education. The author stresses that learners have individual needs and learning characteristics, and they need to be taught accordingly. Teachers have to be able to recognize the skills related to self-determination and know how to teach them. Attitudes are key to the entire process. Students need to have positive attitudes, and as teachers, we need to keep students positive about learning.

Wehmeyer, M. L. (1992b). Self-determination: Critical skills for outcome-oriented transition services. *The Journal for Vocational Special Needs Education, 15,* 3–9. (ERIC Document Reproduction Service No. EJ 452 506)

The author introduces self-determination as necessary to complete the transition process and have a successful vocational education. Vocational, special, and regular educators need to create an environment that fosters self-determination in students with disabilities. Adolescence is a crucial time for students with disabilities to acquire self-determination skills; unfortunately most adolescents with disabilities are in an overly structured environment.

A survey conducted with 254 women and men with disabilities showed that most individuals wanted a different job but were not using self-advocacy skills to get one. These individuals were waiting for someone to give them one. Five strategies were named to promote self-determination: (1) Teach skills promoting self-regulation, (2) emphasize psychosocial skills needed in the work place, (3) structure environments to ensure opportunities for choices, (4) organize instruction to promote self-determination, and (5) use teaching strategies that promote self-determination. Long-term employment stability is the goal of these strategies for people with disabilities.

Wehmeyer, M. L. (1994). Perceptions of self-determination and psychological empowerment of adolescents with mental retardation. *Education and Training in Mental Retardation and Developmental Disabilities, 29* (1), 9–21. (ERIC Document Reproduction Service No. EJ 481 505)

This study examined the psychological empowerment of youth with cognitive disabilities. Locus of control, perceptions of self-efficacy, and outcome expectancies of adolescents with cognitive disabilities ($n = 282$) were evaluated, and differences between a subset of this sample ($n = 52$), adolescents with learning disabilities ($n = 25$), and youth at risk for failure ($n = 26$) were determined. Results of the two studies provide some evidence that students with cognitive disabilities may experience perceptions of psychological empowerment that are not conducive to becoming self-determined, including perceptions of overreliance on luck and chance. These students may have unrealistic perceptions of causality and external perceptions of control. The author suggests that limited opportunity to experience control and choice may be contributing factors to the findings.

Wehmeyer, M. L. (1995). A career education approach: Self-determination for youth with mild cognitive disabilities. *Intervention in School and Clinic, 30*(3), 157–163. (ERIC Document Reproduction Service No. EJ 497 549)

This article addresses identifying self-determination as an educational outcome and the educator's role in providing an effective program to promote these skills in students with and without disabilities. The latter portion of the article gives an overview of the *Life Centered Career Education* (LCCE) curriculum and discusses how the LCCE can be used to promote self-determination. This curriculum, designed for youths with disabilities, provides school, home, and community-based issues that must be addressed to prepare students to assume adult roles.

Wehmeyer, M., & Berkobien, R. (1991). Self-determination and self-advocacy: A case of mistaken identity. *TASH Newsletter, 18*(7), 4.

The terms *self-determination* and *self-advocacy* are sometimes used interchangeably. The authors discuss the relationship of the terms. The process of self-determination includes autonomy, self-actualization, and self-regulation. Self-advocacy is a component of self-determination and is defined as a manifestation of self-regulation, and to a lesser extent, autonomy. Self-advocacy organizations and the concerns and frustrations of those involved are discussed.

Wehmeyer, M. L., & Metzler, C. A. (1995). How self-determined are people with mental retardation? The national consumer survey. *Mental Retardation, 33*(2), 111–119. (ERIC Document Reproduction Service No. EJ 503 000)

Well-developed self-determination skills are necessary to have a successful transition from school to adult life. Research was conducted to identify how self-determined people with cognitive disabilities perceive themselves. The survey consisted of 79 questions in 6 sections: (1) Eligibility and Screening, (2) Demographics, (3) Service Satisfaction, (4) Independence, (5) Integration, and (6) Productivity. Of the 4,544 respondents, 3,365 identified cognitive disabilities as a primary diagnosis and 758 as a secondary diagnosis. The respondents with disabilities perceived themselves as having fewer choices and less control of their lives than people without disabilities. It was found that they had choices for small decisions, such as what to wear, but were not consulted for major decisions, such as whom to have as a roommate. People with cognitive disabilities were generally not taking part in activities that signify adulthood, such as marriage.

Wehmeyer, M. L., & Ward, M. (1995). The spirit of the IDEA mandate: Student involvement in transition planning. *The Journal for Vocational Special Needs Education, 17*(3), 108–111. (ERIC Document Reproduction Service No. EJ 506 036)

This article discusses how the transition from school to work requirements in IDEA must be based on a student's needs, interests, and abilities. It focuses on increasing the participation and planning by individuals involved in the transition services and explains why this is important. The article provides information about what self-determination is and how students with disabilities should have these skills in order to be successful in life after high school. It also provides valuable information about how student involvement in transition planning can be promoted.

Weimer, B. B., Cappotelli, M., & DiCamillo, J. (1994). Self-advocacy: A working proposal for adolescents with special needs. *Intervention in School and Clinic, 30*(1), 47–52. (ERIC Document Reproduction Service No. EJ 489 532)

This article discusses the special education program of the Gates Chili Central School District (Rochester, NY). The authors provide detailed information about the importance of self-advocacy skill instruction and how the district has made a commitment to teaching these skills to students with learning disabilities. The middle school program focuses on awareness of one's disabilities and how modifications can assist one in compensating. This process involves gaining knowledge of the actual process of arranging for modifications and ensuring that all students individually receive the test modifications. The high school program focuses on assisting students to independently use these adult skills through applications and experiences.

West, M., Kregel, J., Getzel, E. E., Zhu, M., Ispen, S. M., & Martin, E. D. (1993). Beyond Section 504: Satisfaction and empowerment of students with disabilities in higher education. *Exceptional Children, 59,* 456–467. (ERIC Document Reproduction Service No. EJ 463 967)

University and college students with disabilities were surveyed to determine their levels of satisfaction with accessibility, special services, and accommodations at their schools. Survey respondents were 761 Virginia college students. Findings suggest that students with disabilities continue to experience barriers in their higher education programs as well as concerns registered with physical accessibility. Students report that they have encountered resistance and discrimination from instructors and other university personnel. Greater percentages of students in 2-year colleges indicated that they were reasonably or very satisfied with their institutions. Many institutions of higher education were found to have only a single full-time or part-time position devoted to arranging or providing an array of services for large numbers of students. Coordinators were found to depend often on volunteers to perform essential and legally mandated services. Authors recommend that (a) institutions of postsecondary education should develop creative means of publicizing the rights of students with disabilities and promote self-advocacy for these students and (b) students with disabilities and their families should be empowered with knowledge of Section 504 and the mandated obligations of institutions of postsecondary education to provide access, services, and accommodations. Support groups and clubs for students with disabilities were often described as a high-priority need.

Wille-Gregory, M., Graham, J. W., & Hughes, C. (1995, Spring). Preparing students with learning disabilities for success in postsecondary education, *Transition Linc,* pp. 1–7. (ERIC Document Reproduction Service No. ED 384 186)

The number of students with disabilities attending postsecondary education has tripled since 1978, and students with learning disabilities now comprise 25% of all of these students. The authors contend that self-determination is a key construct in empowering students to participate in postsecondary education. The authors identify and discuss several materials designed to increase the self-determination of students with learning disabilities. This monograph discusses the educational strategy I-PLAN (Bos & Vaughn, 1991); the *ChoiceMaker Self-Determination Transition Curriculum* (Martin & Marshall, 1995); and *Tools for Transition* (Aune & Ness, 1991). A comparison of IDEA, Section 504, and the Americans with Disabilities Act is also included.

Yuan, F. (1994). Moving toward self-acceptance: A course for students with learning disabilities. *Intervention in School and Clinic, 29*, 301–309. (ERIC Document Reproduction Service No. EJ 483 527)

A course titled *Understanding Learning Disabilities* is described in this article. There are three general goals in this course that deal with basic questions about learning disabilities, learning styles, strengths and weaknesses, and self-advocacy skills. The course is taught to groups of 10 to 12 students. Each class offers information in diverse forms and teaches a three-step self-advocacy procedure. It starts with a positive statement, states the problem, and offers solution strategies. This course is recommended for use in post-secondary programs serving adolescents and young adults with learning disabilities. The results have been positive and encouraging.

Zigmond, N. (1990). Rethinking secondary school programs for students with learning disabilities. *Focus on Exceptional Children, 23*, 1–22. (ERIC Document Reproduction Service No. EJ 421 415)

Statistics indicate a 145% increase in the number of children identified and served as having learning disabilities, with secondary school students representing the largest increase. The author suggests that despite a growing awareness of the needs of students with learning disabilities, current special education programming fails to improve their literacy skills or prevent their dropping out of school. The article recommends concentrating change efforts on controllable elements in school and students. The author outlines four necessary components in effective programming for the adolescent with a learning disability: (1) intensive instruction in reading and mathematics; (2) explicit instruction in "survival" skills; (3) successful completion of courses required for high school graduation; and (4) explicit planning for life after high school. The article also describes two models of delivery—one appropriate for college-bound students, the other suited to learners with minimal skill competency.

CEC Teacher Resources

A Practical Guide for Teaching Self-Determination
by Sharon Field, Jim Martin, Robert Miller, Michael Ward, and Michael Wehmeyer
This practitioner's guide targeted to K-12 special education teachers/special population instructors, work experience coordinators, vocational assessment personnel, guidance and other support staff sets forth the relationships among career development, transition, and self-determination. The book provides detailed reviews of over 30 curriculum materials and assessment tools in the area of self-determination. Practical guidelines educators can use to support self-advocacy and empowerment are included.

      No. P5231, 1997, 178 pp.   ISBN 0-86586-301-6
      Regular Price $39.95   CEC Member Price $27.50

Reducing Disproportionate Representation of Culturally Diverse Students in Special and Gifted Education
Edited by Alfredo J. Artiles and Grace Zamora-Duran
Provides new perspectives for working with children from different cultural backgrounds. Suggests alternative ways to assess and teach culturally diverse students who have behavioral problems, other disabilities, and those who are gifted.

      No. P5219, 1997, 104 pp.   ISBN 0-86586-297-4
      Regular Price $26.95   CEC Member Price $18.95

Disruption, Disaster, and Death: Helping Students Deal with Crises
by Festus E. Obiakor, Teresa A. Mehring, and John O. Schwenn
This one-of-a-kind resource leads the way in providing a candid look at the problems related to situations that involve disruption, disaster, and death and offers a wide array of resources and practices to help students cope with these events. The content is appropriate for general education, but the book also contains sections on how children with exceptionalities may be specifically affected.

      No. P5190, 1997, 120 pp.   ISBN 0-86586-289-3
      Regular Price $26.95   CEC Member Price $18.95

Crossover Children: A Sourcebook for Helping Children Who Are Gifted and Learning Disabled, Second Edition
by Marlene Bireley
A rich resource that provides specific strategies to help children who are gifted and learning disabled and/or ADD control impulsivity, increase attention, enhance memory, improve social skills, and develop a positive self-concept. It also provides recommendations for academic interventions and enrichment activities.

      No. P5121, 1995. 94 pp.   ISBN 0-86586-264-8
      Regular Price $28.00   CEC Member Price $19.60

Tough to Reach, Tough to Teach: Students with Behavior Problems
by Sylvia Rockwell
Through the use of anecdotes, the author prepares teachers for the shock of abusive language and hostile behavior in the classroom. This book will allow you to have a plan for meeting the challenges of teaching these students more effective ways to communicate. Provides many practical management strategies for defusing and redirecting disruptive behavior.

      No. P387, 1993. 106 pp.   ISBN 0-86586-235-4
      Regular Price $24.00   CEC Member Price $16.80

Assess for Success: Handbook on Transition Assessment
by Patricia L. Sitlington, Deborah A. Neubert, Wynne Begun, Richard C. Lombard, and Pamela J. Leconte
Helps the IEP team decide what to assess and how assessment data should be collected and used within the context of career development. Case studies illustrate how this concept applies to students with different levels of ability and different career visions. Provides strategies for assessing self-determination skills.

      No. P5155, 1996. 136 pp.   ISBN 0-86586-281-8
      Regular Price $30.00   CEC Member Price $21.00

Prices may change without notice.
Send orders to: The Council for Exceptional Children, Dept. K80150, 1920 Association Drive, Reston, VA 20191-1589. 1-888-CEC-SPED.